MULTICULTURAL EDUCATION

SOURCE BOOKS ON EDUCATION
(VOL. 18)

GARLAND REFERENCE LIBRARY
OF SOCIAL SCIENCE
(VOL. 355)

SOURCE BOOKS ON EDUCATION

MULTICULTURAL EDUCATION
A Source Book

Patricia G. Ramsey
Edwina Battle Vold
Leslie R. Williams

GARLAND PUBLISHING, INC. • NEW YORK & LONDON
1989

Library of Congress Cataloging-in-Publication Data

Ramsey, Patricia G.
  Multicultural education.

  (Garland reference library of social science ;
vol. 355). Source books on education ; vol. 18)
      1. Intercultural education—United States. I. Vold,
Edwina Battle. II. Williams, Leslie R., 1944–   .
III. Title. IV. Series: Garland reference library of
social science ; v. 355. V. Series: Garland reference
library of social science. Source books on education ;
vol. 18.
LC1099.3.R35 1989   370.19′6   88-31061
ISBN 0–8240–8558–2 (alk. paper)

Printed on acid-free, 250-year-life paper
Manufactured in the United States of America

In Memory of Richard

CONTENTS

PREFACE

This source book contains essays and annotations on a number of issues related to multicultural education. The authors define multicultural education as a process-oriented creation of learning experiences that foster awareness of, respect for, and enjoyment of the diversity of our society and world. Inherent in this definition of multicultural education is a commitment to create a more just and equitable society for all people. Multicultural education, therefore, is relevant to all children, all teaching and curricular decisions, and every aspect of educational policy.

The concept of multicultural education has evolved over the past 20 years. From the desegregation and the ethnic studies movements of the 1960s and 1970s emerged a recognition that all children must learn to live in a diverse world. In the middle 1970s the term "multicultural education" began to appear in the literature as educators articulated its definition and implications for teaching practice. Because this volume is focused on multicultural education rather than its antecedents, the literature annotated in this volume includes materials published during and after 1976.

Bilingual education is closely tied to multicultural education in both philosophy and practice. There is a wealth of resources in this area including policy statements, curricula, and teaching guides. Because there is already an excellent resource book on this topic, Bilingual Education: A Sourcebook, by Alba N. Ambert and Sarah E. Melendez, the essays in this volume do not specifically address bilingual education, and the annotations do not include materials related primarily to bilingual education.

The scope of this book includes theoretical, research, and practical information related to the implementation of a multicultural perspective in early childhood and elementary school classrooms. The first two chapters reflect the authors' conviction that effective multicultural education must be grounded in an understanding of its relation to other social and political movements and in an ability to make curriculum developmentally

appropriate. Chapter I is a description of the philosophical
roots of multicultural education and the socio-political context
of its evolution. The second chapter reviews research on the
development of children's awareness and understanding of racial,
cultural, and social class differences. The next two chapters
discuss applications of multicultural education in educating
children and preparing teachers. Chapter III describes the range
of curricula, programs and teaching strategies designed for early
childhood and elementary classrooms and offers several ways of
categorizing and evaluating them. The annotations include only
programs following most closely the definition of multicultural
education that has guided the writing of this book. Chapter IV
reviews policies and guidelines of multicultural teacher education
and discussses its implementation as described in case studies and
evaluations. Each chapter includes goals specific to its
particular area of multicultural education. In the final chapter,
the authors review and elaborate these goals and discuss the
possible future directions of multicultural education. Chapters I
and IV are relevant to multicultural education in all institutions
and at all ages. Chapter II and III are more specifically focused
on the early childhood and elementary years.

While the primary focus of this book is the multicultural
education movement in the United States, some materials from other
countries, specifically the United Kingdom, Canada, and Australia
are included. Annotations are limited to materials that are
written in English and are available to readers in this country,
so they do not include ones from non-English speaking countries.
References were identified through a number of searches including
ERIC, PSYCHINFO, and Library of Congress. While the essays cover
all topics related to multicultural education described above, the
annotations are limited to ones that reflect the orientation
defined in the introductory paragraph of this preface. To insure
accessibility, annotations are also limited to books and articles
that are available in print. Unpublished dissertations, research
reports, and government documents are not annotated.

Each chapter consists of an essay reviewing the major issues,
historical changes, and related research in its topical area, and
between 30 and 50 related annotated sources. The annotations are
organized alphabetically in each chapter and include full
publication information. In Chapter III, they also are arranged
in the four major categories of programs, curricula, teaching
strategies, and learning materials. Each annotation consists of a
brief summary of the major points of the resource and a commentary
on how it relates to the major issues of the field. In some
cases, specific suggestions about how a resource might be used are
also included.

Authors of books and articles about multicultural education often comment on the lack of adequate terms to describe diversity in a manner that embodies respect for each group, yet acknowledges the reality of past and present discrimination. The authors of this volume, likewise, struggled to find terms that reflected a multicultural perspective, and were forced to make many compromises. After much reflection, we decided to use the term "minority" to refer to racial and ethnic groups that traditionally have been excluded from equal educational, social, economic, and political arenas in American society. The term is not meant to demean or devalue the members of these groups, but rather to critique the power differential that exists between these groups and those who are in control. We also recognize that, in terms of global demographics, this term is inaccurate because groups that have been viewed as "minority" comprise a greater proportion of the world's population than do the "majority" whites. In discussions of other societies, we have used the term "minority" to refer to the groups that have the same status in their countries as "minorities" have in ours, even though their actual ethnic origins may be different. We hope that as a multicultural perspective becomes more pervasive in our schools and society, our language will change so that words that convey diversity will no longer connote deficiency and inferiority.

Multicultural Education

CHAPTER I

THE EVOLUTION OF MULTICULTURAL EDUCATION:
A SOCIO-POLITICAL PERSPECTIVE

Edwina Battle Vold

An historical review of educational movements in the
twentieth century reveals a continuing effort to respond to racial
and ethnic disparities in society. The recent educational
movement in the United States that emphasizes a multicultural
perspective was precipitated by the social unrest of the 1960s.
     This chapter examines the evolution of this multicultural
perspective and the socio-political atmosphere through which it
has evolved. It emphasizes publications which describe the
social, political, and educational policies from which it received
much of its impetus. Although much of the chapter traces the
evolution of this multicultural perspective in the United States,
the literature reviewed reveals similarities in the evolution of
the multicultural perspective in other western societies.

The Evolving Multicultural Perspective

     Education in America has traditionally been dominated by a
monocultural perspective reflecting the assimilationist values of
the larger society. This system of education has excluded the
values, customs, history, and access to power of racial and ethnic
"minority" groups in society, especially people of color.
     The assimilationist ideology in the United States is more
easily recognized as the "melting pot" theory. The concept of the
"melting pot" originated with Israel Zangwill's play, performed on
Broadway in 1909. One of the characters says:

3

> America is God's crucible, the great Melting Pot where all
> races of Europe are melting and reforming! Here you stand,
> good folk, think I, when I see them at Ellis Island, here you
> stand in your fifty hatreds and rivalries, but you won't be
> long like that, brothers, for these are the fires of Irishmen
> and Englishmen, Jews and Russians--into the Crucible with you
> all! God is making the American ... The real American has
> not yet arrived. He is only in the Crucible, I tell you--he
> will be the fusion of all races, the common superman
> (Zangwill, 1907, p. 37).

The underlying assumption was that immigrants of Anglo-Saxon
background and other racial and ethnic groups would mix and result
in a superior new American model. The mix was successful to a
great extent with white immigrant groups from Western Europe.
However, there were immigrants from non-western societies and
groups indigenous to this hemisphere that did not and could not
mix. Thus, the melting pot theory of assimilation became a myth
perpetuated by the dominant social and political groups in
society.
     Periodically during the 20th century, vocal minority groups
challenged the melting pot ideology. They also challenged the
pervasive monocultural education perspective in schools which
perpetuated the melting pot or assimilationist ideology. Changes
have occurred, but not without a social and political struggle.
The educational changes took the form of intergroup education,
ethnic studies, and, more recently, multicultural education.
These changes are called educational movements, and they seem to
parallel social movements. The parallel social movements were
either in response to, or were the cause of, educational changes
in the United States. The beginnings of the educational movements
can be easily chronicled; however, there seem to be no identifiable endings. The educational movements tend to overlap, and now
in the late 1980s features of each of the educational changes and
the monocultural education perspective can be found in elementary
and secondary schools in the United States. The monocultural
education perspective is visible in ideology and practice in many
schools (see Figure 1).

Intergroup Education Movement

     Following World War I, there was a need to establish a sense
of national belonging and loyalty, and to have people identify
with the traditions of America as a country rather than with the
traditions of the country from which they or their ancestors had
immigrated. With the rise of totalitarian regimes and the
apparent threat to democracy, it became important for Americans to

Figure 1

THE EVOLUTION OF EDUCATIONAL ATTITUDES AND PRACTICES
TOWARD CULTURAL PLURALISM IN THE UNITED STATES

Williams & Vold

Phases	Characteristics
The "Melting Pot" 1900 -	- Monocultural Education dominated schools - Orientation to the ideal of "E pluribus unum" - Focus on assimilation - Curriculum content/strategies drawn from classic disciplines (Western European tradition)
The Push Toward "Anglo Conformity" 1920 -	- Monocultural Education dominated schools - Focus on acculturation and similarity - Curriculum drawn from classic disciplines and/or orientation toward preparation for citizenship and loyalty
Toward Desegregation 1950 -	- Intergroup Education was promoted - Pressure to eliminate the "separate but equal" doctrine - Focus on racial balance and institutional change rather than curriculum
Toward Ethnic Revitalization 1965 -	- Ethnic Studies Education as separate courses or subjects - Recognition of the validity of the minority and ethnic experiences - Focus on acknowledgement of differences - Curriculum content/strategies drawn from the history and traditions, and the issues affecting particular ethnic/cultural groups
The Recognition of Cultural Pluralism 1975 -	- Multicultural approach to education appears - Diversity of cultural heritage seen as source of the nation's strength - Focus on balance between similarities and differences - The promotion of curriculum drawn from integration of multicultural perspectives throughout all subject areas

emphasize the strengths of similarities in values, customs, and beliefs. Thus, during this time there was a push for conformity that demanded immigrants completely renounce their ancestry in favor of values and behaviors of the dominant Anglo-Saxon group in the United States. This attitude had a major impact on American society that culminated with the end of World War II, when being an American meant being the best in the world.

As World War II ended, there was growing racial discord in American society, despite the national sense of loyalty and belonging. This racial discord was the result of many historical factors, and was fueled with a new black American sense of purpose brought about by the participation of "Negro soldiers" in the war. These Negro soldiers had fought to make the world free and safe for democracy, yet were relegated to second-class status upon their return to the United States.

With the rising sense of expectations of the Negro soldiers, their demands to be treated better, and their desires for a more equal share of the pie, competition between whites and other racial groups for housing and employment occurred. In response to this heightened period of conflict and tension, schools were called upon to increase interracial understanding. This was the beginning of the Intergroup Education movement.

Intergroup Education was a national project directed by Hilda Taba and designed for elementary and secondary schools. Its instructional activities included the teaching of isolated units on various ethnic groups, exhortation against prejudice, the organizing of intergroup get-togethers, and the banning of books considered stereotypic or demeaning to racial minority groups. A basic assumption of Intergroup Education was that respect and acceptance of another racial or ethnic group could occur as the result of factual knowledge gained (Banks, 1981).

In other societies outside the United States, similar movements of unrest and discontent have affected the educational programs designed for children. These countries include Canada, the United Kingdom, and Australia. In each of these societies, the schools responded with programs designed to silence racial and ethnic protest while increasing, to some measure, the academic success rate of these racial and ethnic groups.

Their educational programs were very much like the Intergroup Education movement in the United States, which failed to become institutionalized though it was widely used in urban schools. Banks posits six reasons why the Intergroup Education movement failed:

1. Mainstream American educators never internalized the ideology and major assumptions on which Intergroup Education was based.

2. Mainstream educators never understood how the Intergroup Education movement contributed to the major goals of American schools.
3. Most American educators saw Intergroup Education as a reform project for schools that had open racial conflict, and tension and not for what they considered their smoothly functioning and nonproblematic schools.
4. Racial tension in the cities took more subtle forms in the 1950s. Consequently, most American educators no longer saw the need for action designed to reduce racial conflict and problems.
5. Intergroup Education remained on the periphery of mainstream educational thought and developments and was financed primarily by special funds. Consequently, when the special funds and projects ended, the movement largely faded.
6. The leaders of the Intergroup Education movement never developed a well articulated and coherent philosophical position that revealed how the Intergroup Education movement was consistent with the major goals of American schools and with American values (Banks, 1988, p. 9).

Ethnic Studies Movement

Around the early 1960s, black Americans and other ethnic groups began to assert their identities differently than had been seen during the period following the Second World War. There were riots and evidence of racial tension between blacks and whites and between the economically advantaged and the economically disenfranchised. There was a refusal to succumb to the myriad of federal and state agencies--social, economic, and educational-- which defined socialization as acquiescence and deculturalization (Bernier & Davis, 1973). With increased awareness of inequities in the areas of work, housing, and education, there were demands to end overt discrimination and segregation. "Black Pride" and "Black Is Beautiful" were slogans soon adapted by Native Americans and Hispanic Americans. This racial pride soon turned to ethnic pride and spilled over into white ethnic groups who brought to reality what Dewey had described in the early 1900s as the hyphenated American (Novak, 1971). Jewish-Americans, Polish-Americans, Italian-Americans and Irish-Americans, to name a few, were caught up in this surge of ethnic awareness and pride.

During this period of ethnic revitalization, schools responded by instituting Ethnic Studies (Banks, 1988). There was a shift in curriculum content to reflect the new demands by ethnic groups, and to include their cultural heritage and contributions. The educational curriculum, which had not previously included racial or ethnic minorities, added studies of separate racial and

other minority groups "emphasizing the four F's--Facts, Foods,
Famous People and Festivals" (Boyer, 1985; Cole, 1986).

In colleges and universities, the curriculum was also
affected by the revitalization of ethnic awareness. Minority
Studies programs were instituted, and courses in black studies,
Asian studies, and Native American studies were created.
Institutes and departments of minority studies were also formed.
These efforts were designed to redress the acknowledged
educational inequities and to respond to the demands of vocal
subgroups who were challenging higher education to eliminate
racism. Although laudable, the curricula were restrictive and
were an addendum to an already prestructured curriculum (Vold,
1979).

During the late 1960s as schools were being desegregated and
integration in the public and private sectors was occurring,
Ethnic Studies began to lose some of its appeal. It had been a
strong educational movement, but it had its limitations, which
were threefold. One, it was content-oriented or knowledge-based
and was often perceived to be divisive. Ethnic groups separated
into courses to study their own cultural contributions and values
to the exclusion of any other group. Two, it was not designed to
deal with causal factors, such as racism or discrimination.
Three, it failed to denounce the perceptions of Anglo-Saxon
ethnocentrism and superiority. Despite its limitations and short
life, the Ethnic Studies movement did have a significant impact on
education in that it served as a primary stage for developing
awareness and appreciation for contributions of black Americans
and other racial and ethnic groups who had been excluded from the
traditional monocultural educational programs. It represented an
attempt to provide students with a more realistic and relevant
curriculum of American society (Boyer, 1985; Foerster, 1982).

Multicultural Education Movement

During the middle of the 1970s, there was another shift in
the social and political perspective which had an impact on
education. Many minority groups, along with disenfranchised black
Americans, were finding that the promised full participation into
mainstream American society had not come about, and neither their
language, customs, nor values were prized. They demanded change
and more control of all institutions, including schools which
affected their lives and those of their children. They also
denounced all ideologies which supported assimilation as
unattainable and undesirable. In its place, black Americans and
other groups advocated cultural pluralism. The response to this
new concept of pluralism was multicultural education. It was
neither an "add on" curriculum nor compensatory in design. Its

purpose was to sensitize all individuals toward ethnic and racial differences, and to increase individual awareness of cultural traditions and sociological experiences. It was also to help all individuals understand that their race and culture, including language and socialization experiences, had value, and could and should exist on a coequal basis with mainstream American values and experiences.

Cultural pluralism was not a new concept in the United States. It had its beginnings in the early 1920s. Horace Kallen, a philosopher, was one of its first proponents. His theory of cultural pluralism attempted to show that America's pluralistic nature was its attraction and strength. He denounced the Anglo conformity ideology and the melting pot theory, and was convinced that Americans could live in several cultural environments, moving in and out freely from group to group. Pluralism was fluid; not designed for the tribalization of society, but designed to provide unity through diversity (Kallen, 1924). Kallen's cultural pluralism did not emerge as a dominant social ideology, nor did it have an impact on the system of education in the 1920s.

In its original form, cultural pluralism, though philosophically sound, was developed without racial and ethnic groups such as black Americans, Hispanics or Native Americans in mind. It was created in response to a need to examine the relationship between the dominant society in the 1920s and the ethnic groups such as the Jews, Southern Europeans and Slavs who were immigrating to America. However, in light of the omission of black Americans, Mexican Americans and Native Americans, cultural pluralism had to be redefined in the 1970s. The new meaning of cultural pluralism, espoused by the National Coalition for Cultural Pluralism in 1971, implies that all cultural, racial, and ethnic groups in American society have the right to mutually coexist and have the freedom to maintain their own identities and lifestyles while providing for their future existence within the confines of the dominant culture (Stent, 1973). Its new meaning is much more inclusive and ideologically appropriate for multicultural education. Several authors provide a thorough discussion of cultural pluralism as a social and philosophical ideology (Itzkoff, 1969; Stent, 1973; Baptiste, 1979; Banks, 1988).

Some authors have expanded the definition of cultural pluralism by the National Coalition for Cultural Pluralism. One interpretation of cultural pluralism is found in an editorial statement by William Hunter. He describes American society as a molecule--it has properties and characteristics unique to its substance, and it exists only as long as its atoms are working together to maintain its existence. Each of the atomic units preserves its own unique characteristics, but the larger molecular structure does not survive without its contributing atoms (Hunter,

1973). Another interpretation of pluralism was developed by Ramirez and Castaneda (1974), called cultural democracy. Their cultural democracy assumes that persons have legal as well as moral rights to remain identified with their own ethnic group, values, language, home, and community, as they learn of and accept mainstream values.

Cultural pluralism or cultural democracy remains the unifying element in multicultural education. As such, it must be evident in the philosophical statements of schools, colleges, and universities, and, more importantly, in the implementation process. In Grant's (1978) description of the process of implementing a multicultural education program, cultural pluralism is inherent in his four features:

1. Staffing patterns and compositions throughout the organizational hierarchy reflect the pluralistic nature of American society.
2. Curricula are appropriate, flexible, unbiased, and incorporate the contributions of all cultural groups.
3. Affirmation of the languages of cultural groups is based on different rather than deficit theories.
4. Instructional materials are free of bias, omissions, and stereotypes; are inclusive rather than supplementary; and show individuals from different cultural groups portraying different occupational and social roles (p. 47).

A study of education in other western cultures, such as the United Kingdom, Canada, Sweden, and Australia, reveals similar developmental trends toward multicultural education in schools, and cultural pluralism as a social ideology. Though the societal changes toward cultural pluralism and concurrent educational changes toward multicultural education may have occurred in different time frames from those in the United States, we find that the sequence of the developmental stages seems to be invariant. The changes in education in other countries begin with the emphasis on intergroup education or human relations and move to a period of ethnic awareness and then to a more inclusive educational movement called multicultural education (Modgil, 1986) or multiculturalism (Bullivant, 1986; Lee, 1983; Samuda, 1986) or interculturalism (Friesen, 1977). In addition to the similarities in the sequential development of educational movements, all of the countries reflect demographic changes by migration or immigration. The impetus for the educational reform, like that in the United States, was motivated by the political need to reduce the hostility and alienation toward the migrants or immigrants.

Multicultural education in the United States and in other western countries is not always clear as to its intention. Nor do

the skeptics feel that an educational movement like multicultural
education can bring about understanding between groups. There are
other concerns, too. There is fear that there is a tendency to
trivialize the concept of multicultural education. There are
concerns that multicultural education has become a synonym for
minor curriculum changes to accommodate the demands and/or needs
of minority groups without addressing the problems of racism. In
some countries and in some schools in the United States,
multicultural education is seen as education for all, not for
minorities only. Others see it as a necessary process in the
education of all ethnic groups, including whites. This, however,
is not a universal belief or practice. Too often, multicultural
education in the United States and other countries is seen as a
program to emphasize the exotic differences of minority groups.
To prevent multicultural education from being trivialized and its
purpose distorted, however, its advocates must clarify its meaning
and provide teachers appropriate models for implementation (Verma
& Bagley, 1984).

Clarifying the Meaning of Multicultural Education

The multicultural education movement has suffered much
criticism since its inception in the early 1970s. Attempts to
gain full acceptance have been hampered by confusion and debate
over the meaning of multicultural education, its philosophical
basis, and its viability as a process for bringing about equity in
society. According to Banks (1986), this confusion and debate
should be expected. He states:

> (Since) multicultural education ... deals with highly
> controversial and politicized issues such as racism and
> inequality (it) is likely to be harshly criticized during its
> formative stages because it deals with serious problems in
> society and appears to many individuals and groups to
> challenge established institutions, norms and values. It is
> also likely to evoke strong emotions, feelings and highly
> polarized opinions. As it searches for its raison d'etre,
> there is bound to be suspicions and criticisms (p. 222).

Much suspicion has centered around what critics call the lack
of clarity in terminology and the lack of a conceptual framework
(Verma & Bagley, 1984; Vold, 1979). Although the authors of this
book use the term multicultural education, we are cognizant of
other terms, such as multiethnic education, education that is
multicultural, intercultural understanding, and multiracial

education, which have similar meanings and conceptual frameworks. Terminology drives definitions; however, the authors of this book found few conceptual variations in meaning between the definitions of multicultural education in the United States and in other countries. From the various definitions, three underlying themes evolve: the definitions generally accept cultural pluralism as the underlying ideology, the definitions reject the melting pot or assimilationist ideology, and the definitions emphasize content and process as elements necessary for program implementation.

The basic document from which all of the definitions of multicultural education in the United States evolve is the "No One Model American" statement adopted in 1972 by the American Association of Colleges for Teacher Education (AACTE). It states that multicultural education:

> ... values cultural pluralism. It rejects the view that schools should seek to melt away cultural differences or the view that schools should tolerate cultural pluralism. Instead, multicultural education affirms that schools should be oriented toward the cultural enrichment of all children and youth through programs rooted to the preservation and extensions of cultural alternatives... Multicultural education recognizes cultural diversity as a fact of life in American society, and it affirms that this cultural diversity is a valuable resource that should be preserved and extended... Multicultural education reaches beyond awareness and understanding of cultural differences. More important than the acceptance and support of these differences is the recognititon of cultural differences and an effective education program that makes cultural equality real and meaningful (AACTE, 1973, p. 264).

Multicultural education was defined by the National Council for the Accreditation of Teacher Education (NCATE) in its standards as early as 1977. It defines multicultural education as a process of preparing individuals for the social, political and economic realities which they will and do experience in culturally diverse and complex human encounters. Through this process, the individual develops competencies for perceiving, believing, evaluating, and behaving in differential cultural settings to become more responsive to the conditions of all humans, the cultural integrity of the individual and the diversity of the society (p. 14). This definition of multicultural education is used by all colleges and universities with teacher education programs as a criterion in the evaluation and accreditation process.

There are many variations of the above definition which have surfaced since the AACTE statement, "No One Model American".

Although there are more variations and definitions in the literature than could be included in this chapter, we have selected six definitions/types to be highlighted: Multicultural Education, Ethnic Studies, Intercultural Education, Multicultural Studies, Multiracial Education, and Education that is Multicultural. A more extensive review of multicultural education definitions can be found in an article by Sleeter and Grant (1987). They have developed a typology of multicultural education which includes the categories of: Teaching the Culturally Different, Intergroup Studies (human relations), Single Group Studies, Multicultural Education, and Education that is Multicultural and Social Reconstructionist.

Multicultural education is the most frequently used term in the United States (AACTE, 1972; Baker, 1979; Dolce, 1978; Gollnick & Chinn, 1983; Gold & Grant, 1977; NCATE, 1974; and Ramsey, 1987). The authors who use this term seem to support Baptiste and Baptiste (1970) in their definition of multicultural education as the transference of the recognition of a pluralistic society into a system of education. They further regard it as a philosophy and a process that guides the total education enterprise. At its most sophisticated level, it exists as a product, a process, and a philosophical orientation guiding all who are involved in the educational enterprise.

In defining the goals for multicultural education in the United Kingdom, Lynch (1983) defines multicultural education as:

> the initiation of children into critical-rational acceptance of cultural diversity and the creative affirmation of individual and group difference within a common humanity. That means that it is a process conducted according to explicit, rational evaluative criteria: an ethical process, celebrating both diversity and unity, social differentiation and cohesion, stability and deliberate, systematic and evaluated changes according to explicit yardsticks, themselves the subject of critical discourse (p. 14).

Multicultural studies has been used in the literature on multicultural education. Although James Boyer uses the term multicultural studies, he gives equal attention, as does Baptiste, to content and process as essential elements which must be drawn from the historical and sociological heritage of various ethnic groups. This approach addresses the similarities, as well as the differences, within the framework of equal respect for these traits. Its purpose is to fill the void created by the long exclusion of cultural, racial, and ethnic minority groups (1985).

Multiethnic education is probably the next most widely used term in the literature next to multicultural education. Many of its definitions are derived from the statement posited by the

National Council of the Social Studies (1976). Two of the most
widely read advocates of multiethnic studies are James Banks and
Geneva Gay. Banks (1988) describes ethnic studies as an
educational process concerned with modifying the total educational
environment to reflect the ethnic diversity of American society.
This includes the study of ethnic cultures and the necessary
changes in the educational environment to ensure equal educational
opportunity for all.

Education that is multicultural is a creation of an early
advocate of the multicultural perspective. Grant rejects the term
multicultural education because he thinks that multicultural is an
adjective which delimits the meaning and suggests a speciality, as
opposed to the totality of one's education. Thus he believes that
when education supports cultural diversity and individualized and
personalized differences, it is not limited or restrictive; it
pervades the total curriculum and the total school environment
(1978). Grant's latest publication (1987), coauthored with
Sleeter, expands his concept of Education that is Multicultural to
include Social Reconstructionist. The change in the phrase was
designed to underscore the emphasis that should be placed on
social action, and challenged the existent social structural
inequality (1985, 1987). This approach suggests more emphasis on
helping students gain a better understanding of oppression and
inequality, and ways in which social problems can be eliminated
(Suzuki, 1984). This approach reflects the new emphasis the
United Kingdom is placing on racism reduction. New literature
from the United Kingdom utilizes the terminology Anti-racist in
place of multicultural education.

There are other advocates of multicultural education who find
the term multicultural education limiting and prefer to emphasize
the social action and structural inequality which exist in society
(Sarap, 1986; Katz, 1980). Sarap (1986) says that the term
Multiracial Education is preferred to multicultural education in
that it conceptually addresses the issue of institutionalized
racism. Since race is controversial and arouses anger, pride, and
often guilt, multicultural education is too soft a term in its
connotation to deal with issues of race and structural power.
Multiracial education brings these to the forefront and highlights
issues of discrimination and differences in access to resources in
power which eventually affect the lives of minorities who are
disenfranchised.

Intercultural education is a term used in some educational
programs in other western societies with culturally diverse
populations. In Canada, this term is used to describe a content-
type of process which emphasizes patterns of beliefs and
behaviors, values and mores of minority peoples. Since minority
cultures are the main focus of the educational curricula, there
tends to be more attention given to compensatory education, or an

Ethnic Studies approach, which was prevalent in American schools during the 1960s and early 1970s (Friesen, 1977).

Underlying the differences in terminology and definitions are some conflicting issues that are being raised as multicultural education comes of age. One issue is whether multicultural education should include gender, class, and the handicapped. Since they were not a part of the original goals of multicultural education, there is a fear that such expansion diffuses the original purpose of multicultural education (Gay, 1977). Other issues which have caused conflict involve the belief that multicultural education is a divisive tool. According to critics, it reinforces and extends the already existing myths and stereotypes propagated on society's ethnic and racial groups.

Another issue confronting multicultural education lies in its expected outcomes. A projected outcome of multicultural education is to help students develop the ability to make reflective decisions so that they can resolve personal problems, and, through social actions, influence public policy and develop a sense of political efficacy (Banks, 1988). Herein lies the problem raised by the social reconstructionists. Does multicultural education in its present form help students gain and develop social and political efficacy? If it does, what results should we expect? Will the results of multicultural education pose a threat to the existent power group? These same questions were raised in the 1960s when the social ideology in the United States was being challenged. What will be the outcome of this Civil Rights movement? If black Americans and other minorities develop social and political efficacy, will the outcome be social and political leadership locally? nationally?

Multicultural education, if it is to be brought to fruition, must have as its outcome constructive change toward social and political, as well as educational, equity. Inherent in any of the definitions must be the equal sharing of power and control in a given society. For a society that talks of its pluralistic nature, values, and equity on one hand, and demands conformity and practices to a set of values and beliefs on the other, the true implementation of multicultural education will be an impossible task, and in reality an educational deception perpetuated on society.

Multicultural Education and Public Policies

Since the Civil War, significant legislation affecting race and the rights of all Americans has occurred. However, it was the Brown v. Board of Education of Topeka, Kansas in 1954 that most

directly affected discriminatory educational practices against
black Americans. Specifically, it is considered the most
significant legislation since the 15th Amendment, which granted
all Americans the right to vote. The Civil Rights Act of 1964 was
also significant in that it consisted of Titles VI and VII which
prohibited discrimination on the basis of race, color, and
national origin in schools and places of employment receiving
federal funds (Hiatt, 1981). It is seen as the major attempt of
the federal government to establish a national policy
acknowledging the coexistence and rights of all groups in society.

Other legislation in the twentieth century which had an
impact on the response of schools to racial and ethnic diversity
includes Title VII of the Elementary and Secondary Education Act.
This 1972 legislation provided grants for bilingual education
programs, along with Title IX of the Ethnic Heritage Studies Act,
which explicitly advocated the study of minority cultures by all
students, and the Lau v. Nichols court decision which validated
the language of Chinese Americans in San Francisco, and the right
to use their language as an educational tool to acquire equal
access to education and economic success. The Lau v. Nichols
decision was expanded in 1980 to include all children whose native
language was other than English. This expanded ruling by the
Department of Education has since been rescinded by the Reagan
Administration (Serow, 1983).

The policies on bilingual education received much of their
impetus from the research of Ramirez and Castaneda (1974). Their
research showing the importance of language and the cognitive
learning styles in the development of appropriate learning
environments was a real breakthrough for bilingual education as
well as multicultural education. The issue of language also
stimulated the emergence of multiculturalism in Canada (Samuda,
1986). Giles and Gollnick (1977), Hiatt (1981) and Serow (1983)
offer their readers a significant review of legislative policies
which promote, however remotely, the multicultural perspective.

The literature on multicultural education in culturally
diverse societies reveals an ongoing debate as to the existence or
nonexistence of multicultural education policies, how the policies
were established, and to what extent they are effective. A most
widely read source of these debated issues is found in Modgil, et
al. (1986).

In certain countries like the United Kingdom, multicultural
policies are in official government documents or in action plans
(Bullivant, 1986). Other countries like the United States have no
specific multicultural education policy. The United States,
however, can point to the Constitution, court decisions, and
legislative acts as examples of policies which promote the
multicultural perspective. However, as Grant (1977) writes, if

one is to study the philosophy underlying these documents while at
the same time studying the social, economic, and educational
practices in the United States, a tremendous gap is revealed
between the intent of the documents and the practices which
perpetuate racial and ethnic inequities in schooling and
employment.

The closest the United States has come to establishing a
specific multicultural education policy was in 1965 with the
enactment of the Ethnic Heritage Studies Act. It authorized
schools to provide all children with the opportunity to study
racial and ethnic minority groups in the United States. As a
result of this act, schools, colleges, and universities received
monies to develop and implement supplementary educational
materials on racial and ethnic minority groups. Other policies
which followed were the National Defense Education Act and the
International Education Act which made provisions for students to
study in other countries in order to bring about mutual
understanding and cooperation between nations. In the early
1970s, the federal government passed a legislative act, entitled
The Emergency School Aid Act, that authorized activities and
short-term institutes related to the culture and heritage of black
Americans, as well as the development of new curricula and
instructional methods to support educational programs for children
from diverse groups. All of these legislative acts, which can be
characterized as policies, were not intended to provide quality
education for children, but were politically motivated and
designed to bring about social and economic stability (Giles &
Gollnick, 1984).

During this same decade, 1965-1975, the Australian government
established a multicultural education policy to equalize the
education of its immigrants and females. Although there had been
much resistance to this educational change, and to the move toward
equity of immigrants and females, there was a growing awareness
that if the policy was to be implemented successfully, there
needed to be involvement of immigrants and females in the decision
making (Harvey, 1987).

The overall focus of the national policy was to promote
equity, tolerance, and participation within a culturally
pluralistic society. It specifically advocated the teaching of
cultural and linguistic heritages of ethnic minorities, the
development of culturally appropriate curricula, the study of
cohesion and unity, and intercultural education. There were,
however, no specifics on how individual schools were to deal with
issues of equity, or how to ensure accountability. The Australian
government, according to some educators, was advocating its public
policy, while, at the same time, creating bureaucratic committees
to advise the government on multicultural issues and women's
issues. These committees provided citizens with a false

impression that change was occurring when, indeed, the committees
were camouflaging the lack of commitment to the policies and the
government's attempt to maintain the existent social structure of
the society (Harvey, 1987).

The importance of involving all constituents at the
bureaucratic level is evident in the White Paper-Red Paper debate
which occurred in Canada in the late 1960s. The White Paper was
issued by the federal government of Calgary as a policy statement
on the way to solve the problems of the Canadian Indian community
and how the government expected to deal with this minority group.
The paper stated that:

> the policies proposed recognize the simple reality that the
> separate legal status of Indians and the policies which have
> flowed from it had kept the Indian people apart from and
> behind other Canadians ... Thus the intent was to remove
> barriers which impede the development of people of regions
> and of the country (Freisen, 1977, p. 164).

The White Paper further pointed out that every cultural group in
Canada is capable of making a rich contribution to Canadian
society and that this should be encouraged, especially with regard
to Indian people. Examples of this rich contribution included the
history, the traditions and the art forms of Indian life. Speech,
language, and folklore were listed, but without adequate
information to give teachers ideas as to what was meant by them
(Freisen, 1977).

The Indian leaders in Alberta responded to the White Paper
with what is known as the "Red Paper". The Red Paper rejected
many of the policy statements of the White Paper. A primary
reason for the rejection of the policy was that there was no
collaborative venture; no discussion with Indian leaders had
occurred. In other words, policies, laws, and regulations
regarding Indians should seek involvement of the constituents who
are to be affected. As one Canadian noted in A Discussion
Handbook for the Indian People: Choosing a Path, a document
developed by the Indian Affairs Branch in 1968:

> ... although the promise to the Indian people was an attempt
> to grant them equal opportunity to expand and develop their
> identity, it did not take into account the differences
> between Indian values and goals and the values and goals of
> the dominant society (p. 2).

A paper by Samuda (1986) describing multicultural policies in
Canada emphasizes non-British and non-European immigrant groups
and their attempts to obtain equity. Samuda's paper reveals the
changing demographics of Canada with its immigrant groups who

arrived between 1960 and 1970, but does not deal with the issues
and concerns for the equity of the Indians who claim to be the
first inhabitants. Freisen (1977), on the other hand, emphasized
Canadian attempts to provide equity to Indians, Hutterites, and
Mennonites.

There exists since 1970, however, a government statement on
multiculturalism in Canada. It recognizes the existence of two
languages; it accepts cultural pluralism as the underlying
framework of a multicultural society; it represents a concern for
a protection of the civil and human rights of people of different
racial, ethnic, and cultural origins; and it rejects the Anglo
conformity, bigotry, racism, and ethnocentrism that formed the
basis of government practice and intercultural relations in Canada
in the 1950s and 1960s.

Several authors have described the different multicultural
policies. They include: Baker (1979), Garcia (1979), Verma et
al. (1984), and Watson (1979). Keith Watson's article (1979) is
of particular interest because he does a comparison of educational
policies in multicultural societies and provides the reader with
an analysis of differences in the policies and how they are used.
He has categorized multicultural societies and their policies into
three groups: (a) countries with deep-rooted social mixes, (b)
countries which were originally colonized, and (c) so-called
democratic countries.

Watson points out that educational policies within societies
with indigenous social mixes, such as the Soviet Union, India, and
China, have used their policies to resolve education problems
created by the socially diverse groups. These countries
decentralize the power and administration of the educational
rights of minority social groups to individual provinces, states,
or republics. In countries or societies which have been
influenced by colonialism, like many of the third world countries,
the educational policies have been used to maintain social and
political dominance of the ruling class. Societies such as the
United States and Canada, which have been transformed as the
result of immigration, have traditionally advocated educational
practices designed to deculturalize its immigrants, according to
Watson (1979). The governmental policies of these countries prior
to the 1970s leaned very heavily toward assimilation. In the
opinion of Garcia (1979), however, the United States and Canada,
in spite of the early assimilation policies have developed some
strong reactions against assimilation, and since 1970 have
advocated a policy of cultural pluralism.

In the review of national policies and multiculturalism,
there is evidence that some countries have policies and others do
not. Based upon much of the literature on race, ethnicity, and
education, the United Kingdom has dealt with multicultural
education more extensively than any other country since 1977. The

United Kingdom has announced publicly its position to meet the
educational needs of its minority children, and has spent
considerable time clarifying its policy and attempting to
transform its policy into action. However, James Lynch, a
well-known educator and multicultural advocate, thinks there has
been government apathy and sluggish inactivity in the United
Kingdom. He thinks schools and teacher centers, rather than the
government, have been in the forefront of developing appropriate
curricula for a culturally diverse society. He also thinks that
recent publications in the United Kingdom are advocating a
holistic approach to multicultural education, and these
publications provide teachers with ways they can plan and
implement curricula responsive to immigrant children and other
minority groups (Lynch, 1983).

Although there is no federal multicultural education policy
in the United States, there are specific educational policies at
the national level, and from state departments of education, that
are publicly acceptable. NCATE, for example, has a multicultural
education policy which must be addressed by member colleges and
universities. "No One Model American" (AACTE) provided the
earliest policy statement, which is reflected in policy statements
of other professional educational organizations, such as The
National Council for Social Studies (NCSS). The NCSS policy on
multicultural and multiracial education provides guidelines and an
evaluation tool for teachers and administrators at the secondary
level. In some states, such as Michigan and Pennsylvania,
policies governing the implementation of multicultural education
come from state departments of education and, in some cases, local
school districts. Schools in states like Michigan are encouraged
to include in their curriculum individuals and contributions
representative of America's cultural, racial, and ethnically
diverse population (Baker, 1977). In the United States, state or
local education agencies provide inservice teacher training for
teachers on multicultural education curricula. At the state and
local levels, legislators and school boards have provided
guidelines which were designed to meet the intent of multicultural
education. However, because legislative guidelines are not rules
or regulations, many state departments of education, as well as
administrators at the local level, have found that they have no
way of addressing the problems of noncompliance.

Summary

Multicultural education evolved in the early 1970s but not in a vacuum. Social transformations of societies, brought about by racial and ethnic groups, by migrant or immigrant groups who tended not to fit into an assimilationist model, have contributed to the shift toward a multicultural perspective. This shift has been in response to social, economic, and political needs rather than educational needs of children. In fact, the purpose of a multicultural perspective which is to provide educational equity for all children has yet to be realized.

Multicultural education policies, where they have been developed, have also been political in nature as societies have attempted to solve social and/or educational problems inherent in changing demo- graphics. In the United States, except for federal legislation supporting components of multicultural programs, there has been no national consensus to provide a national policy of multicultural education. Other western countries with culturally diverse populations seem to be far ahead of the United states in providing policies which ensure multicultural practices.

Multicultural education is going through growing pains; it is constantly convincing society of its raison d'etre, and has become a source of unending debate. There are those who think that it represents an attempt to politicize education in order to pander to minority group demands, while other critics think it is a racist device used by the dominant group to exploit ethnic groups in order to maintain white middle class control, dominance, and insensitivities (Parekh, 1986). Although it is still developing, multicultural education is slowly approaching maturity. If the current trend in the United States toward a return to assimilation and Anglo conformity continues, its effectivess for future generations will be questionable. On the other hand, if multicultural education proponents prevail and provide theoretically sound concepts and practical ways to implement them, the future of multicultural education will be effective and productive in providing equity in schools and in building an equitable and democratic society.

References

Baker, Gwendolyn C. "Policy Issues in Multicultural Education in the United States." _Journal of Negro Education_ 48(3) (1979): 253-66.

Banks, James A. _Education in the 80's: Multiethnic Education_. Washington, DC: NEA, 1981.

Banks, James A. _Teaching Strategies for Ethnic Studies_. Boston: Allyn & Bacon, Inc., 1987.

Banks, James A. _Multiethnic Education: Theory and Practice_. Boston: Allyn & Bacon, Inc., 1988.

Banks, James A. "Multicultural Education and its Critics: Britain and the United States." _Multicultural Education: The Interminable Debate_. Edited by Sohan Modgil, Gajendra Verma, Kanka Mallick, and Celia Modgil. London: The Falmer Press, 1986.

Baptiste, H. Prentice, Jr. _Multicultural Education: A Synopsis_. Washington, DC: University Press of America, Inc., 1979.

Bernier, Normand R., and Richard H. Davis. "Synergy: A Model for Implementing Multicultural Education." _Journal of Teacher Education_ (1973): 286.

Boyer, James B. _Multicultural Education: Product or Process?_ Kansas City, KS: Kansas Urban Education Center, 1985.

Boyer, James B., and Joe L. Boyer (Eds.). _Curriculum and Instruction After Desegregation: Form, Substance and Proposals_. Manhattan, KS: Ag. Press, 1975.

Broudy, Harry S. "Cultural Pluralism: New Wine in Old Bottles." _Educational Leadership_ 33 (1975): 173-75.

Bullivant, Brian. "Towards Radical Multiculturalism."
    Multicultural Education: The Interminable Debate. Edited by
    Sohan Modgil, Gajendra Verma, Kanka Mallick, and Celia
    Modgil. London: The Falmer Press, 1986.

Bullivant, Brian. Pluralism: Cultural Maintenance and Evolution.
    Clevedon, Avon, England: Multilingual Matters, Ltd., 1984.

Choosing A Path: A Discussion Handbook for the Indian People.
    Ottawa: Indian Affairs Branch, 1968.

Clothier, Grant, Anne R. Gayles, Larney G. Rackley, and Sandra W.
    Rackley. New Dimensions in Multicultural Education. Kansas
    City, MO: Mid-West Educational Training & Research
    Organization, 1978.

Cole, Mike. "Teaching and Learning about Racism: A Critique of
    Multicultural Education in Britain." Multicultural
    Education: The Interminable Debate. Edited by Sohan Modgil,
    Gajendra Verman, Kanka Mallick, and Celia Modgil. London:
    The Falmer Press, 1986.

Foerster, Leona. "Moving from Ethnic Studies to Multicultural
    Education." The Urban Review 14 (1982): 121-26.

Foster, Lois, and David Stockley. Multiculturalism: The Changing
    Australian Paradigm. Clevedon, Avon, England: Multilingual
    Matters, Ltd., 1984.

Friesen, John W. People, Culture and Learning. Calgary, Alberta:
    Destselig Enterprises Ltd., 1977.

Garcia, F. Chris. "Politics and Multicultural Education Do Mix."
    Journal of Teacher Education 3 (1977): 21-25.

Gay, Geneva. "Multiethnic Education: Historical Developments and
    Future Prospects." Phi Delta Kappan 64 (1983): 560-63.

Giles, Raymond, and Donna Gollnick. "Ethnic/Cultural Diversity as
    Reflected in State and Federal Educational Legislation and
    Policies." Pluralism and the American Teacher: Issues and
    Case Studies. Edited by Frank Klassen and Donna Gollnick.
    Washington, DC: AACTE, 1977.

Glazer, Nathan, and Daniel Moynihan. Beyond the Melting Pot.
    Boston: MIT Press, 1970.

Glazer, Nathan. "Ethnicity and Education: Some Hard Questions."
    Phi Delta Kappan 64 (1983): 386-89.

Gold, Milton J., Carla A. Grant, and Harry Rivlin, (Eds.). In Praise of Diversity: A Resource Book for Multicultural Education. Washington, DC: ATE, 1977.

Gordon, Milton, (Ed.). Ethnic Groups in American Life Series. Englewood Cliffs, NJ: Prentice-Hall, 1971.

Grant, Carl A. Multicultural Education: Myth or Reality." Unpublished paper. Madison, WI: University of Wisconsin, 1977.

Grant, Carl A. "Education That is Multicultural--Isn't That What We Mean?" Journal of Teacher Education 29 (1978): 45-49.

Greenbaum, William. "America in Search of a New Ideal: An Essay on the Rise of Pluralism." Harvard Educational Review 44 (1974):

Harvey, Jim. "Ethnicity and Gender in Australian Education." Unpublished paper presented at AERA, Washington, DC, 1987.

Hess, Robert D., and Doreen Croft. Teachers of Young Children. Boston: Houghton Mifflin Co., 1972.

Hiatt, Dana. "The Law of Minorities in the United States from 1620 to 1980." Perspectives in Multicultural Education. Edited by William Sims and Bernice Boss de Martinez. New York: University Press of America, 1981, 17-51.

Hunter, William A. "Cultural Pluralism: The Whole is Greater than the Sum of its Parts." Journal of Teacher Education 24 (1973): 262.

Itzkoff, Seymour W. Cultural Pluralism and American Education. Scranton, PA: International Textbook Co., 1970.

Ivie, Stanley D. "Multicultural Education: Boon or Boondoggle?" Journal of Teacher Education 30 (1979): 23-25.

Kallen, Horace. Culture and Democracy in the United States. New York: Boni and Liveright, 1924.

Krug, Mark. "Cultural Pluralism: Its Origins and Aftermath." Journal of Teacher Education 28 (1977): 5-9.

Lee, Mildred K. "Multiculturalism: Educational Perspectives for the 1980's." Education 103 (1983): 405-9.

Lynch, James. The Multicultural Curriculum. London: Batsford Academic and Educational Ltd., 1983.

Modgil, Sohan, Gajendra Verma, Kanka Mallick, and Celia Modgil,
    (Eds.). Multicultural Education: The Interminable Debate.
    London: The Falmer Press, 1986.

"No One Model American: A Statement on Multicultural Education."
    Journal of Teacher Education 24 (1973): 264.

Novak, Michael. The Rise of the Unmeltable Ethnics. New York:
    Macmillan, 1971.

Pratte, Richard. "Multicultural Education: Four Normative
    Arguments." Educational Theory 33 (1983): 21-32.

Protinsky, Ruth Anne. "Multicultural Education: An Historical
    Overview." Society, Culture, and Schools: The American
    Approach. Edited by Hunt and Whitehurst. Maryland: Garrett
    Park Press, 1979.

Ramirez, Manuel, and Alfredo Castaneda. Cultural Democracy,
    Bicognitive Development and Education. New York: Academic
    Press, 1974.

Ramsey, Patricia G. Teaching and Learning in a Diverse World:
    Multicultural Education for Young Children. New York:
    Teachers College Press, 1987.

Samuda, Ronald. "The Canadian Brand of Multiculturalism: Social
    and Educational Implications." Multicultural Education: The
    Interminable Debate. Edited by Sohan Modgil, Gajendra Verma,
    Kanka Mallick, and Celia Modgil. London: The Falmer Press,
    1986.

Sarap, Madan. The Politics of Multicultural Education. London:
    Routledge and Kegan, 1986.

Serow, Robert C. Schooling for Social Diversity: An Analysis of
    Policy and Practice. New York: Teachers College Press,
    1983, pp. 93-95.

Sleeter, Christine E., and Carl A. Grant. "An Analysis of
    Multicultural Education in the United States." Harvard
    Education Review 57 (1987): 421-44.

Standards for the Accreditation of Teacher Education. Washington,
    DC: NCATE, 1982.

Stent, Madelon D., William R. Hazard, and Harry Rivlin. Cultural
    Pluralism in Education: A Mandate for Change. New York:
    Appleton-Century Crofts, 1973.

Taba, Hilda, Elizabeth Hall Brady, and John T. Robinson.
    Intergroup Education in Public Education. Washington, DC:
    American Council on Education, 1952.

Verma, Gajendra K. and Christopher Bagley (Eds.). Race Relations
    and Cultural Differences. London: Croom and Helm, 1984.

Vold, Edwina B. (1979). "Multicultural Perspectives." Society,
    Culture and Schools: The American Approach. Edited by Hunt
    and Whitehurst. Garrett Park, MD: Garrett Park Press, 1979.

Watson, Keith. "Educational Policies in Multicultural Societies."
    Comparative Education 15 (1979): 17-31.

Zangwill, Israel. The Melting Pot. New York: Macmillan, 1907.

Bibliography

1. Baker, Gwendolyn C. "Policy Issues in Multicultural Education in the United States." _Journal of Negro Education_ 48(3) (1979): 253-66.

   The author explores the issues related to the development of policy having an influence upon multicultural education. She looks at the impact of local initiative on policy which seems to occur in local areas in response to racial discontent and disruption. She further identifies legislative efforts of some states and where states require multicultural education only in some schools, without thought that multicultural education is as important for the "non-minority" child as for the "minority" child. She reports in her article that "In 1979, the Commission Report from AACTE revealed that 68 percent of the states had passed legislation, promulgated regulations and guidelines, and developed policy. Most of the educational activity toward multicultural education that was identified during the seventies, Baker says, was the result of legislation and policy enacted at the state level. The author supports lobbying for multicultural education which, she says, has not been well developed by educators.

2. Banks, James A. _Multiethnic Education: Theory and Practice_ second edition. Boston: Allyn & Bacon, Inc., 1988.

   This is Banks second edition of a 1981 textbook. Its five parts are similar to those in the earlier work in that it includes sections on the history, goals and practices in multiethnic education, conceptual issues and problems related to culture and ethnicity, the philosophical and ideological issues related to education and ethnicity, curriculum, and finally, a section on teaching strategies.

27

For the reader with limited knowledge of the history of
multicultural education in the United States, Banks' section
I is thoroughly researched and clearly written for the
novice or experienced multicultural education proponent.

3. Banks, James A. Teaching Strategies for Ethnic Studies.
        Boston: Allyn & Bacon, Inc., 1987.

        Although Banks' book is a textbook for preservice and
inservice teachers who teach ethnic studies, chapter one
provides the reader with definitive descriptions of
multicultural education, ethnic studies, multiethnic
education, and global education, and the goals and
objectives of each. The chapter provides startling
statistics on the immigrant/minority patterns in the United
States, which should provide teachers with data affecting
education and social economic patterns.

4. Banks, James A. "The Social Studies, Ethnic Diversity, and
        Social Change." The Elementary Journal 87 (1987).

        Banks describes the goals of the ethnic revival
movement throughout the Western world. He outlines how
educational circles in countries such as the United States,
Canada, Great Britain, and Australia responded to the ethnic
revival period following the Black Civil Rights Movement of
the 1960s. There is evidence provided that curriculum
changes that occurred during this period tended to
trivialize the very ethnic cultures they were designed to
enhance. He provides a review of the literature, which
gives idealogical reasons for resistance to multicultural
education.

5. Baptiste, H. Prentice, Jr. Multicultural Education: A
        Synopsis. Washington, DC: University Press of
        America, Inc., 1979.

        The text provides a broad view of multicultural
education, from its evolution to issues related to bilingual
education. The history of multicultural education in the
United States provided by the author gives additional data
not often found in the historical development of
multicultural education. The synopsis has selected

. annotations of multicultural education resources, and a
glossary of terms is provided.

6. Boyer, James B. Multicultural Education: Product or
Process? Kansas City, KS: Kansas Urban Education
Center, 1985.

The author provides the reader with a description of
the multicultural education approach. He deals with the
prevailing definitions of multicultural education and how it
developed. Within the developmental phases, he describes
legislative efforts which attempted to resolve difficulties
resulting from racial and ethnic inequities in educational
systems in the United States. The author provides a
multicultural education model which engages both product and
process, and discusses multicultural education parameters
which extend beyond the compensatory approach of earlier
multicultural educational approaches.

7. Broudy, Harry S. "Cultural Pluralism: New Wine in Old
Bottles." Educational Leadership 33 (1975): 173-75.

The author examines the subtle differences between
cultural pluralism as purported by Horace Kallen in 1924 and
the new concept of cultural pluralism of the mid 1960s to
1970s. The author intimates that cultural pluralism which
denotes separatism is more prevalent today, whereas cultural
pluralism in the early 1900s purports unity in diversity.
One's philosophical beliefs about cultural pluralism
determine the types of educational policies that are put
into place. His interpretations are based on generalized
assumptions about what current cultural groups who press for
cultural pluralism want, and on his historical perspective,
seventy years later, on the intentions of Kallen.

8. Bullivant, Brian. "Towards Radical Multiculturalism."
Multicultural Education: The Interminable Debate.
Edited by Sohan Modgil, Gajendra Verma, Kanka Mallick,
and Celia Modgil. London: The Falmer Press, 1986.

Throughout the chapter, Bullivant argues the issue that
multiculturalism and pluralism as concepts related to the
type of schooling provided for ethnic and racial minorities
is faulty. He sees the terms as utopian in thought with
little reality of how they are supposed to deal with power
and the conflicts which are caused by race, class and

gender. He feels that a multicultural curriculum does
nothing to enhance the "equality of educational opportunity
and life-chances" of racial and ethnic minority children.
He proposes an ideology which he purports is much more
politicized and power-sensitive. He calls it radical
multiculturalism and indicates it needs more discussion to
provide the reader with an understanding of its structural
framework.

9. Bullivant, Brian. Pluralism: Cultural Maintenance and
        Evolution. Clevedon, Avon, England: Multilingual
        Matters, Ltd., 1984.

        The author points to several themes throughout the
    book. His most poignant theme deals with the nature of
    power and control and the dangers inherent in acceptance of
    a pluralistic ideology. He provides in the first half of
    his book a description of how pluralism evolved historically
    in response to economic and political changes and pressures
    in the social system. He provides the pitfalls and
    potentials for pluralism in other Western societies in the
    final chapter. His revelations regarding the Australian
    Aborigines serve as a model of how cultural groups can
    resist assimilation and gain access to social and economic
    resources.

10. Clothier, Grant, Anne R. Gayles, Larney G. Rackley, and
        Sandra W. Rackley. New Dimensions in Multicultural
        Education. Kansas City, MO: Mid-West Educational
        Training & Research Organization, 1978.

        The first two chapters by Clothier provide a
    description of the historical development of a social and
    political atmosphere adapting to the tide of immigrants
    during the nineteenth and twentieth centuries. It is clear
    that the authors feel that the educational system bears part
    of this responsibility. His rationale for multicultural
    education provides the reader with an overall purpose,
    interwoven with the opinions and writings of several
    proponents of multicultural education. One conclusion,
    however, is that, given that we live in a multicultural
    society, there is a discrepancy between our ideals and our
    practices.

11. Foerster, Leona. "Moving from Ethnic Studies to
         Multicultural Education." The Urban Review 14 (1982):
         121-26.

         This article highlights the pitfalls that brought about
    the diminishment of the ethnic studies movement. Though
    ethnic studies were popular in the 1970s, they had some
    limitations that caused the movement to wane. First, there
    was the lack of commitment of teachers, who had little time
    to prepare thoroughly for its implementation. Second, the
    teachers' guides for ethnic studies did not provide teachers
    with a sufficient knowledge base, rendering the
    implementation of the program ineffective. Third, the lack
    of input from teachers may have caused difficulty in
    implementation and teacher negativism. Fourth, ethnic
    studies was added on to, rather than infused into the
    existing curriculum. Fifth, there was an inability to
    resolve the controversy over what should be included in the
    curriculum, who the curriculum should be for and when the
    curriculum should be implemented. The sixth, and last,
    identified limitation was the lack of community support.
    Multicultural education, which the author describes as the
    replacement to ethnic studies, is a stronger concept than
    multiethnic studies. To ensure that multicultural education
    does not follow the path of multiethnic studies, the author
    reiterates the causal factors of multiethnic education's
    doom in a positive framework. It is her position that
    multicultural education can succeed and endure if we can
    demonstrate to a broad constituency that it adds a viable
    dimension to the education of all students.

12. Foster, Lois, and David Stockley. Multiculturalism: The
         Changing Australian Paradigm. Clevedon, Avon, England:
         Multilingual Matters, Ltd., 1984.

         This small book offers an historical interpretation of
    multiculturalism in Australia. It provides a theoretical
    framework by which the reader can analyze the development of
    the present status of multiculturalism. The second and
    third chapters read like a chronicle of Australian events
    which take us from the early twentieth century into the
    1980s and through various government leaderships. The final
    chapters provide the reader with an assessment of the
    effectiveness of the concept of multiculturalism in
    Australia and the development and assumption underlying the
    multicultural policy. Through the use of case studies, the
    authors weave a rather dismal picture of the penetration of
    multiculturalism into education, the media and law. They

conclude that there are hidden structures such as the logic
of Australian capitalism and its accompanying ideology in
conjunction with other external factors related to class and
social power which impede the effective implementation of
multicultural policy.

13. Friesen, John W. People, Culture and Learning. Calgary,
        Alberta: Destselig Enterprises Ltd., 1977.

        The central theme of this book is intercultural
education. The author provides a basis for analyzing the
meaning of intercultural education by giving it an
interdisciplinary framework from the fields of anthropology,
ethnology, sociology, and psychology. The history of
intercultural education is portrayed concomitantly with the
social and economic development of the Canadian Indians, the
Hutterites, and the Mennonites within a pluralistic setting.
The conflicts inherent in the assimilation of groups into
Canadian society are highlighted.

14. Gay, Geneva. "Multiethnic Education: Historical
        Developments and Future Prospects." Phi Delta Kappan
        64 (1983): 560-63.

        In her article on the historical development and future
prospects of multiethnic education, Gay weaves a descriptive
picture of the beginnings of multiethnic education and the
sociopolitical atmosphere which prevailed from the late
1960s into the 1980s. She also expounds on the criticisms
levied against multiethnic education from inside and outside
the educational community. She concedes that multiethnic
educational goals have expanded, and that multicultural
education has grown into conceptual maturity. However, she
warns proponents of the danger of broadening the scope of
multicultural education to include experiences of women, the
handicapped, the aged, and the poor. The author thinks
that, with certain cautionary procedures, there is a future
for multiethnic education, though it may be uncertain and
less politically motivated.

15. Glazer, Nathan. "Ethnicity and Education: Some Hard
        Questions." Phi Delta Kappan 64 (1983): 386-89.

        In this critical analysis of the pluralist orientation,
the author discusses the pitfalls of how America responds to

ethnicity. There is a bit of reminiscing about the way it
used to be when immigrants arrived and were quickly
assimilated by the schooling received. He points out the
dangers inherent in seeking policies to support perceived
language barriers of speakers of black English, or
Spanish-speaking immigrants who are divided in their support
of bilingual, bicultural programs. As a critic of
multicultural education, Glazer thinks that valuing cultural
pluralism may be one of the causal factors in the general
decline of self-confidence in the virtues of American
society and its world domination and respect.

16. Gordon, Milton. <u>Assimilation in American Life</u>. New York:
        Oxford University Press, 1964.

        In his book on assimilation in the United States,
Gordon identifies and defines social ideologies: Anglo
conformity, the "melting pot," and cultural pluralism.
Anglo conformity is a philosophic belief that demands that
immigrants completely renunciate their ancestry in favor of
behavior and values of the dominant Anglo-Saxon group. The
"melting pot" concept implies a biological and sociological
merger of cultural groups into a unique American model.
Cultural pluralism argues for the maintenance of unique
identities of cultural groups involved in limited
integration and interaction in political and economic life
in the United States.

17. Grant, Carl A. "Education that is Multicultural--Isn't That
        What We Mean?" <u>Journal of Teacher Education</u> 29 (1978):
        45-49.

        The author posits reasons why eduation that is
multicultural is a more acceptable concept for education in
a racially and culturally pluralistic society than is the
term multicultural education. This work of Grant marks the
beginning of a debate regarding the meaning of multicultural
education. He identifies what he terms the implicit
weaknesses of multicultural education as an educational
concept. However, most of his manifest, implied, and latent
components of education that is multicultural, can be found
in definitions by other proponents.

18. Henley, Richard, and Jonathan Young. "Multicultural
        Education: Contemporary Variations on a Historical
        Theme." <u>The History and Social Science Teacher</u> 17
        (1981).

The article is a description of the recurring themes in
the educational history of Canada and how it has been
influenced by multicultural education policy. The authors
describe the relations between Canada's indigenous groups
and the newcomers and how each is affected by the system of
education. On the other hand, they outline how the system
of education has been affected by the inflow of newcomers
and is called upon to overcome the negative and dangerous
qualities of the newcomers. They also include a more recent
update of the problems of Indian education in Canada.
Leaning heavily on the works of Gibson (1976), the authors
provide a typology of multicultural education which consists
of education of the culturally different or benevolent
multiculturalism, education about cultural differences,
education for cultural pluralism, and bicultural education.
Within this section, the authors provide the reader with a
bibliographic epilogue of contributors to each of these
approaches. These approaches are reflective of the
recurring themes in Canada's educational history as it has
attempted to address the changes in society.

19.   Hollins, Etta Ruth. "Beyond Multicultural Education."
      Negro Education Review 33 (1982): 140-44.

      Hollins provides an abbreviated history of the
development of multicultural education. She then provides
for the reader a view of the relationship between learning
theories. In a precise article, Hollins points out that,
although learning theorists such as Piaget, Skinner, and
Ausubel seem to recognize the significance of culture in how
learning takes place, none seems to embrace the concept of
cultural pluralism. In fact, most seem to be consistent
with the "melting pot" theory. As such, she posits the need
for a multicultural theory of learning.

20.   Ivie, Stanley D. "Multicultural Education: Boon or
      Boondoggle?" Journal of Teacher Education 30 (1979):
      23-25.

      The author reprimands educators for purporting that
multicultural education can solve the basic problems of our
larger society. He feels that if minorities are to gain
equal status in our society, they must receive "quality"
education. Within a relatively short and concise article,
the author raises concerns regarding "the melting pot
metaphor replacement," the lack of definition of

multicultural education. The reader is quick to observe
that the author thinks multicultural education is not equal
to quality education; however, no explanation of quality
education is provided.

21. Jakubowicz, A. "State and Ethnicity: Multiculturalism as
      Ideology." Australian and New Zealand Journal of
      Sociology 17 (1981): 4-13.

      This article examines the ways in which the concepts of
multiculturalism and ethnicity are defined in Australia.
The definitions are used to redefine and redirect the demand
for ethnic rights, according to Foster and Stockley (1984).
The author traces the evolution of policy of assimilation
through multiculturalism which was chosen to replace the
former assimilationist and integrationist policies. In his
opinion, the establishment of multicultural policy was the
means to maintain social control and cultural hegemony by
the dominant Anglo-celtic population, and their vehicle was
through education. His interpretation of the Galbally
Report (1978) differs in substance from that of the
Evaluation Report offering readers a less positive view of
the Multicultural Education Program (M.E.P.).

22. Katz, Judy H. "Multicultural Education: Games Educators
      Play." Integrated Education 18 (1980): 101-4.

      The author points out the realities of racism in
American society and the necessity of multicultural
education as a process which could, but has not, eradicated
these racist attitudes and beliefs. The author delineates
various reasons why multicultural education has remained
more rhetoric than practice. These reasons are outlined as
games which educators play, such as: the definition game,
the tokenism game, the escape game, and the divide and
conquer game. She offers suggestions for preventing
administrators and other policy makers from sabotaging
multicultural efforts and moving toward more substantive
progress.

23. Lee, Mildred K. "Multiculturalism: Educational
      Perspectives for the 1980's." Education 103 (1983):
      405-9.

Lee's article points out that whites are often victims in a racist society just as non-whites are. She believes that if "racism can be perceived as a problem which causes untold economic, psychological, and social damage to both whites and non-whites, perhaps more resources will be applied to combat it." Multiculturalism or cultural pluralism in principle has the potential to repair this damage. There are, however, problems which the author alludes to: 1) the tendency toward conservation and the visibility of reactionary racist extreme groups, 2) the lack of trained teachers prepared to introduce pluralistic materials to all children whether minority group children are in the classroom or not, and 3) the need to reexamine the objectives of schools and to ensure that they are compatible with the goals of multiculturalism. The author point out the schools cannot foster multiculturalism alone. She sees multicultural education--in conjuction with other institutions such as the family, community, and media--as the viable way to reduce racial and ethnic tensions.

24. Lynch, James. "Multiethnic Education in Europe: Problems and Prospects." Phi Delta Kappan 64 (1983): 576-79.

In this article, Lynch chronicles the factors that contribute to a European movement toward multicultural education. The major factor highlighted is the pattern of settlement in Europe where linguistically different groups were in contact with one another.

25. Modgil, Sohan, Gajendra Verma, Kanka Mallick, and Celia Modgil, (Eds.). Multicultural Education: The Interminable Debate. London: The Falmer Press, 1986.

This edited volume has 15 essays that deal with the debate over multicultural education in the United Kingdom, Australia, Canada, and the United States. The contributors seem to agree that there is confusion and contradiction in philosophies, goals, and policies. There is much confusion as to whether multicultural education can eradicate racism or whether it serves to maintain the power structure of society in the hands of its white citizenry. The only contributor and spokesperson for multicultural education in America who has provided answers to some critics from an American point of view is James Banks.

26. Pratte, Richard. "Multicultural Education: Four Normative
        Arguments." Educational Theory 33 (1983): 21-32.

        Normative policy arguments are provided as parameters
     for examining multicultural education. The author attempts
     through these four arguments to provide the reader with a
     logical way to use one or more of the arguments to support
     or negate an educational policy toward diversification based
     on culture or ethnicity. His comparisons of restricted
     argument, unrestricted argument, modified restricted
     argument and modified unrestricted argument, each with three
     premises, provide the reader sufficient data to come to a
     logical conclusion. The arguments are exciting ways to
     examine educational progress, or the lack of it, toward
     multicultural education.

27. Ramirez, Manuel, and Alfredo Castaneda. Cultural Democracy,
        Bicognitive Development and Education. New York:
        Academic Press, 1974.

        In their attempt to affect educational policies which
     affect the learning experiences of children from diverse
     backgrounds, the authors posit a philosophy called cultural
     democracy. One of its goals is to provide a system where
     students from diverse populations can function in two
     cultures. They delve into research on two concepts:
     bicultural identity and bicognitive development. In the
     chapter on the Ideology of Assimilation, the authors
     skillfully describe the myth behind the evolving
     sociopolitical ideologies of the "melting pot" and Anglo
     conformity, and the resulting conflicts they produce in
     Mexican-American students.

28. Samuda, Ronald. "The Canadian Brand of Multiculturalism:
        Social and Educational Implications." Multicultural
        Education: The Interminable Debate. Edited by Sohan
        Modgil, Gajendra Verma, Kanka Mallick, and Celia
        Modgil. London: The Falmer Press, 1986.

        Multiculturalism in Canada represents a radical shift
     on the part of the federal government, and the policy has
     been accepted by four of the ten provinces. It represents a
     recognition of the cultural diversity of Canadian society.
     In other words, cultural pluralism is the essence of
     Canadian identity.

29. Sarap, Madan. The Politics of Multicultural Education.
     London: Routledge and Kegan, 1986.

        Throughout the book, the author adamantly rejects the
     use of the term multicultural education in that it is an
     inaccurate description of what it purports to do. His
     rejection goes further toward eliminating the cultural
     pluralistic ideology, and provides the reader with a strong
     conviction that social arrangements cannot be discussed from
     a psychological level, but from a context of power. It is a
     discussion of the definition of terms; the author rejects
     the term multicultural because the term culture tends to
     ignore economic position and social power. His use of race
     and multiracial education brings to the forefront issues of
     discrimination of blacks and differences in access to
     resources and in power to affect events.

30. Serow, Robert C. Schooling for Social Diversity: An
     Analysis of Policy and Practice. New York: Teachers
     College Press, 1983.

        This book is an examination of educational trends in
     American society which have contributed to changes in
     attitudes and behaviors about diverse groups. The
     historical review of American society's treatment of racial
     and ethnic differences provides the reader with the role
     that schools have played in inculcating these social
     beliefs. The two types of inculcating processes which
     schools have engaged in are described as political
     socialization and racial relations. In Serow's chapter on
     multicultural education, the sections on outcomes for
     students and schools and the outcomes for society provide a
     refreshing approach to the significance of multicultural
     education as a process. It also reiterates the importance
     of the commitment of teachers and administrators in ensuring
     the success of multicultural education. The final chapter
     points out some social and political trends which could have
     a devastating effect on multicultural education in light of
     the conservative social political perspective and the trends
     toward new budget priorities away from social programs.

31. Sims, William, and Bernice Bass de Martinez. Perspectives
     in Multicultural Education. New York: University Press
     of America, 1981.

This book was a product of the Ethnic Studies Heritage
Act, and was designed to increase teachers' awareness of
levels of cultures and lifstyles of individuals who are
culturally different. It is an edited volume which contains
four sections: Foundations of Multicultural Education,
Approaches to Multicultural Education, Teaching Strategies,
and Lesson Plans. The second chapter in Section I deals
with the Law and Minorities in the United States from 1620
to 1980. The contributing author of this chapter, Diana S.
Hiatt, has provided the reader with a precise description of
significant legislative policies and court decisions that
have impacted on the implementation of educational programs
that have a multicultural perspective. The legislation is
inclusive of acts which relate to black Americans, Chinese
Americans, Japanese Americans and Native Americans. Chapter
III, co-authored by Estrada and Vasquez, provides the reader
with controversial issues regarding schooling and its
psychological effects upon minorities.

32. Sleeter, Christine E., and Carl A. Grant. "An Analysis of
     Multicultural Education in the United States."
     Harvard Education Review 57 (1987): 421-44.

     Grant and Sleeter provide the reader with a thorough
review and analysis of literature which addresses
multicultural education from the United States and other
English-speaking countries. The review covers articles
which deal with policy, purposes and goals, models,
curriculum, instructional processes, teacher education,
teaching grades, calls for action, projects, research, and
anti-multicultural education articles. With regard to
policy issues, the authors posit that though articles from
Australia, United Kingdom, and Canada seem to support a
national policy on multicultural education, the mandate for
the United States to adhere to such a policy seems to be
evident. Of interest to most advocates of multicultural
education is the typology of multicultural purposes and
goals. The authors categorized the approaches to education
that are found in the literature into five areas: Education
for the Culturally Different, Ethnic Studies, Human
Relations, Multicultural Education and Education that is
Multicultural and Social Reconstructionist. Their
discussion of the weaknesses of each article and approach
provides much insight into the need for more clarity, more
specificity in ways they are to be implemented, and research
on the outcomes of such conceptual changes in educational
practices in society.

33. Verma, Gajendra K., and Christopher Bagley (Eds.). Race
        Relations and Cultural Differences. London: Croom and
        Helm, 1984.

        In their introduction, the editors take a different
stand from their previous unyielding support of
multiculturalism and pluralism to point out various problem
areas: theoretical construction, practical implications,
and research problems. The evaluation of multicultural
education in Great Britain ranges from laissez faire
assimilationist to a policy of integration. Any support for
multiculturalism is localized within education centers
heavily populated with immigrants. The policies of European
countries--such as France, Sweden, The Netherlands, the
United Kingdom, and Germany--are compared. Findings reveal
that the educational systems in these countries are deeply
rooted in elitist ideologies, making upward mobility nearly
impossible for its immigrants. The multicultural policies
which these governments promote are based on psychological
research which highlights the problems of specific ethnic
groups, counteracts efforts of the proponents of
multiculturalism, and provides reinforcement for policy
makers of multicultural education.

34. Verma, Gajendra K., and Christopher Bagley (Eds.).
        Multicultural Childhood: Education, Ethnicity and
        Cognitive Styles. England: Gower Publishing Company,
        1983.

        In the introductory chapter, the editors have an
extensive discussion which attempts to define and to clarify
pluralism. The contributing authors have some chapters
dealing with cognitive styles (e.g. field dependent vs.
field independent) and socialization processes. The reports
primarily cover research on West Indian students, Jamaicans,
Japanese, the Sikhs, and the Gajarates from South Asia.
Comparative studies are also included.

35. Verma, Gajendra., and Christopher Bagley. "Multicultural
        Education: Problems and Issues." Race Relations and
        Cultural Differences. Edited by Gajendra Verma and
        Christopher Bagley. London: Croom and Helm,
        1984.

In the introduction to their edited volume, the authors illustrate the complexities surrounding the explanation of multicultural education or multiculturalism. The authors selected three problem areas which tend to highlight the concerns raised by proponents and critics alike. The problem areas are theoretical, practical or research in nature. Theoretical concerns center on: 1) the inability to define culture adequately to cover the various traditions and various perspectives perceived by individuals within the culture, and 2) the so-called non-coincidence of culture with national boundaries where different cultures "have differing and sometimes competing claims to political, social and economic resources, power, and representation; these competing claims can be met by responses ranging from racism and class domination to 'consociational' democracy which strives to establish equality between cultures." The practical concerns center on ways to understand the changing society and ultimately the changing educational systems within a framework that promotes political equity. Policy-wise multicultural education is much too localized according to the authors. They point out that there is no national policy valuing multiculturalism, though the rejection of the aspirations of minorities does exist. The research problems center around problems of comparing cultural groups and individuals within cultural groups, and subsequent problems which center around validity and reliability. The authors point out some concerns they have had which have led to a change in their own perspectives. They highlight: 1) the lack of systematic and intellectual studies to combat the rhetoric of unreason accompanying the condemnations of the various models of pluralism, 2) the trivialization of the concept of multicultural education, and 3) the infrequently recognized problem of race relations in North America and Australia. The edited volume is a compilation of updated papers at conferences in Europe and North America.

36. Watson, Keith. "Educational Policies in Multicultural Societies." Comparative Education 15 (1979): 17-31.

The author surveys educational policies which affect ethnic and cultural mixes in European communities, the Soviet Union, India, China, the United States, and Canada. He prefers to examine educational policies by grouping the countries into three broad classification schema: Countries with a deep-rooted social mix, countries influenced by colonialism, and countries whose social mix results from

immigration. It is the contention of the author that
societies with social mixes resulting from immigration are
turning toward a policy of cultural pluralism. The author
purports that education is the most logical vehicle for
implementing government policy toward multicultural
education.

CHAPTER II

ETHNIC DIVERSITY AND CHILDREN'S LEARNING

Patricia G. Ramsey

The effective implementation of a multicultural perspective requires that activities, concepts, and adaptations be appropriate for the specific children in the classroom. Research on the development of ethnic awareness, identity, and attitudes provides helpful guidance for teachers and curriculum developers in their planning of curricula and in their day-to-day decisions about specific activities and strategies. The following discussion is a review of the research that has been done on children's responses to racial, cultural, and social class differences and related educational implications.

Children's racial awareness and related cognitive and affective processes have been studied in a number of different populations and with a wide variety of methods. Because there are so many studies, and the findings and methods are often complex and contradictory, the annotations in this section primarily include reviews of research and chapters that discuss the most salient and consistent findings, rather than individual research reports. In contrast, there have been relatively few studies of children's awareness of cultural and socioeconomic differences, so some specific studies are annotated in these sections.

Although racial, cultural, and class differences are treated separately in this essay, there is considerable interaction and overlap among these attributes. Racial differences are often associated with both cultural and class differences, both in actual circumstances and in the perceptions that people have about their own and other groups (Rex, 1986). Thus, children's responses to these factors are probably more complex and varied than those that are found when they are studied separately.

Children's Responses to Racial Differences

"Race" is used in this section to identify groups that share
discernible physical attributes that traditionally are defined as
racial. This concept, while often used as a biological
distinction, is, in fact, a social label, as is evident in the
inconsistent and biased ways in which racial terms are often
applied. The issue of race has become more complicated with
increasing numbers of interracial births, transracial adoptions,
and immigrants with mixed racial heritage. The following
discussion is written, not in support of the use of racial
distinctions, but in recognition that in many societies, children
grow up in environments where these characteristics are often the
basis for discriminatory behavior. Furthermore, the visible
characteristics associated with racial differences make them more
salient to young children than less concrete differences of social
class and culture.

Types of Research

During the 1940s and 1950s there were a number of studies of
children's racial awareness and attitudes which appeared to
demonstrate the negative effects of segregation and
discriminiation of black children's identity and self concept
development (e.g., Clark & Clark, 1947; Goodman, 1952). These
studies were incorporated into arguments for integrating public
schools in the 1954 Brown v. Board of Education (Topeka, Kansas)
Supreme Court Decision. The research in this period also
paralleled the post World War II intergroup education movement
described in Chapter I by focusing on the development of
intergroup attitudes and possible sources of prejudice. In
Goodman's book (1952), there is an extensive review of the
research during this period.

In the years following the 1954 Supreme Court Decision, a
number of researchers studied the social dynamics of desegregated
schools and the conditions that either fostered or undermined
positive intergroup relationship (e.g., Patchen, 1982; St. John,
1975; Schofield, 1981, 1982; Singleton & Asher, 1977; Slavin,
1980). The attitudes of teachers towards white and black children
were also assessed during this period (e.g., Gottlieb, 1964;
McCandless, Roberts & Starnes, 1972). In the 1970s the
recognition that desegregation did not necessarily lead to
successful integration contributed to the shift towards
multicultural education, and similarly gave rise to increased
research on the complexities of racial awareness and attitudes.
The studies of this period are characterized by a variety of

approaches and multiple methods, as exemplified by Porter's (1971)
study and Williams and Morland's (1976) series of studies. There
are several reviews that organize and summarize this research
(Brand, Ruiz, and Padilla, 1974; Katz, 1976a, 1976b, 1982). In
the 1980s, there have been a number of critiques of earlier
studies that used methods now regarded as too simplistic to
measure the complex processes that make up children's responses to
racial differences (e.g., Aboud & Skerry, 1984; Sigelman &
Singleton, 1986). Findings of the earlier studies that concluded
that black children had poor identities and self concepts have
been challenged for approaching the study of black children from a
deficit orientation (e.g., Cross, 1985, 1987). Recent writers
have also emphasized the need to study and understand minority
children within their own contexts, and not simply to measure them
with the views and methods typically used to study white children.
The recent publication of Beginnings: The Social and Affective
Development of Black Children (Spencer, Brookins, & Allen, 1985)
is an example of this perspective. This orientation to research
reflects the cultural pluralist orientation that underlies the
multicultural education movement. Hale-Benson's (1986) volume on
black children's learning, play, and social styles also embodies
this perspective. In its stress on the distinctiveness of the
Afro-American experience, however, it also reflects the ethnic
studies orientation of the 1970s.

     Despite numerous studies, the knowledge about children's
reactions to racial differences is still incomplete and
fragmented. Most research in this country has focused on
children's responses to blacks and whites. Only recently have
researchers begun to include a broader range of subjects and to
measure children's reactions to other groups, such as Asian or
Hispanic children. Thus, the research by no means offers a
complete picture of children's reactions to all groups. It does,
however, offer some insights into the ways in which children react
to race that are relevant to the implementation of multicultural
education.

     Children's responses to racial differences involve a
complicated set of cognitive, affective, and behavioral dimensions
(Katz, 1976a, 1982; Sigelman & Singleton, 1986). While
development is continuous in all of these dimensions, each process
may be influenced by different learning experiences, so that there
is not complete congruence between cognitive, affective, and
behavioral responses. Rosenfield and Stephan (1981) suggest that
classification skills depend on cognitive development; affective
responses reflect socialization influences such as parents,
siblings, and the media; and behavioral preferences are determined
by situational constraints, such as the amount of contact allowed
with other groups. For instance, children may develop
cross-racial friendships by having contact with individual peers,

yet learn negative attitudes about that group as a whole from
adults. In this case, the behavioral and attitudinal processes
may appear to be in conflict. There is evidence that, with age,
attitudes become more consistent across cognitive, affective, and
behavioral components (Milner, 1983).

Cognitive Dimensions

     Many studies have shown that children notice racial cues
during infancy and, by the age of three or four, most children
have a rudimentary concept of race (Katz, 1976a). Preschool
children can accurately apply socially conventional labels of
"black" and "white" to pictures, dolls, and people, but they are
not necessarily aware of their own ethnic affiliation (Aboud,
1977). The salience of race in children's perceptions of others,
and the kind and amount of information that they learn about
racial differences, varies according to children's social milieu,
their majority or minority status, and the extent and kinds of
contacts they have with other racial groups (Rotheram & Phinney,
1987b). There is evidence that the type of task, also has an
effect on whether or not children notice or remark on racial
differences (Semaj, 1981). Because of their level of cognitive
development, children who are learning about groups often
exaggerate the intergroup differences and minimize the intragroup
ones (Katz, 1976a; Tajfel, 1981).
     During their elementary years, children begin to elaborate
their concepts of race as they begin to associate social
information with the physical attributes that they see (Katz,
1976). As this shift occurs, they rely less on color cues and
begin to grasp the social meaning of racial terms (Alejandro-
Wright, 1985). They also develop a more accurate understanding of
the nature of racial differences. Clark, Hocevar, and Dembo
(1980) identified four levels of children's reasoning about the
causes of racial differences. First, children attribute them to
the actions of a supernatural or powerful being (e.g. "God painted
them that way"). At level two, children use arbitrary reasons
(e.g. "He looks that way because he's got a red shirt on.").
Level three is characterized with relevant, but incorrect,
physical explanations (e.g. "They look that way because they were
born in Africa"). As children approach the middle childhood
years, they are able to provide correct explanations. Analogous
to their reasoning about the causes of differences is their
growing awareness of the immutability of racial characteristics.
Katz (1982) speculates that children may go through a series of
phases parallel to the sequence of gender constancy acquisition
found by Kohlberg (1966). Although there has not been a specific
study of this sequence, there is observational evidence that

preschoolers do not assume that race is a permanent characteristic (Ramsey, 1986a).

Children's racial identity becomes more consolidated during childhood. Preschoolers are often inconsistent when asked whom they look like and frequently make distinctions on nonracial attributes such as hairstyle or clothing. As mentioned previously, some earlier studies found that children of color stated that they were white (Clark & Clark, 1947; Goodman, 1952), and these responses were interpreted as indications that black children wished that they were white and therefore had low self-esteem. In recent critiques of these studies, Cross (1985, 1987) has pointed out that they measured reference group orientation, not personal self-esteem or identity. He suggests that the "misidentification" may be an attempt to resolve the contradiction between feeling personally valued, yet disparaged because of group membership. Studies that have been done after the 1960s suggest that the more positive images of blacks evident in the black community, in schools, and in the media may be reducing this dissonance. Recent studies have found that Afro-American children are more likely to have a black reference group orientation (e.g. Farrell & Olson, 1982; Cross, 1985).

Affective Dimensions

Evaluative concepts, if they are part of a child's environment, are likely to be incorporated into a child's rudimentary awareness of race and to become more consolidated and elaborated with age (Katz, 1976a). Brand et al. (1974) conclude that affective reactions, either positive or negative, are formed at an early age and do not change much as children mature. Variables which may contribute to the formation of ethnic-related attitudes are personality traits (Allport, 1954) and situational factors, such as heterogeneity, and degree of upward mobility (Rotheram & Phinney, 1987b). Children absorb prevailing racial attitudes through direct and indirect instructions by parents, peers, teachers, and contact with printed and electronic media which reflect prevailing stereotypes (Milner, 1983).

Affective responses to racial differences have been typically measured with forced choice tasks in which children are asked to select the doll, puppet, drawing, or photograph that matches certain positive or negative descriptions   (e.g. "Show me the smart boy.")   (e.g. Clark & Clark, 1947; Rohrer, 1977). This method, however, has been criticized (Aboud & Skerry, 1984; Sigelman & Singleton, 1986) because it exaggerates the level of bias and relies on adult-generated distinctions. Children's affective reactions have also been measured with various tests in which children express their preferences for objects colored black and white (Williams & Morland, 1976) or select potential "friends" from a multiracial group of photographs, dolls, puppets, etc.

As with the identity tasks, earlier studies showed a pre-white bias in both black and white children (e.g. Clark & Clark, 1947). For the black children, this pattern may have reflected a dissonance similar to that evident in the identity measures. More recent studies suggest that both whites and blacks show same-race preference (Farrell & Olson, 1982).

Children's friendship choices in multiracial classrooms have also been analyzed for patterns of racially-related preferences. Gender is the strongest predictor of choices, and there is little evidence of same-race preference during the preschool years (Jarrett & Quey, 1983) and early elementary grades (Singleton & Asher, 1977). There is, however, a trend toward increasing racial cleavage during the elementary and high school years (Asher, Singleton & Taylor, 1982; Schofield, 1981).

Racially-related affective responses become increasingly consolidated during the elementary years as preference patterns become more consistent and supported with reasons (Milner, 19834; Porter, 1971). In the late elementary years, attitudes become crystallized (Goodman, 1952; Katz, 1976). This trend, however, is somewhat offset by children's increasing cognitive capacity that enables them to become curious about other groups (Aboud, 1977) and to understand other people's perspectives (Davidson, 1976).

Behavioral Dimensions

There have been relatively few recent studies of children's actual cross-racial behavior, and the findings about younger children appear to be mixed. Porter (1971) and Singleton and Asher (1977) observed few signs of cross-race avoidance or antagonism. Finkelstein and Haskins (1983), however, concluded that the same-race preference that they observed in kindergarteners must also be present in its rudimentary stages during the preschool years.

During the elementary years, there is increasing racial cleavage as children absorb more of the prevailing social attitudes, and the awareness of "us" versus "them" becomes more established (Katz, 1976a). This trend continues, and accounts of inter-racial contacts in middle schools and high schools show how vehemently and explicitly peers discourage cross-race contact (Patchen, 1982; Schofield, 1981). However, there is also evidence that, with sustained cross-group contact, children develop more positive behaviors towards individuals in another group more readily than they change their attitudes towards the group as a whole (Schofield, 1982). One of the most promising areas of research has been the work in creating racially integrated

cooperative learning teams. There is evidence that these
interventions do result in a significant increase in interethnic
friendships (Rosenfield & Stephen, 1981; Slavin, 1980).

Educational Implications

There have been some studies on the question of whether or
not race is a factor in teacher-child relationships, but the
evidence is somewhat contradictory (Kohut, 1980). In general, the
evidence suggests that white teachers are more receptive to white
children than they are to black children. Earlier studies found
that white teachers had more negative feelings about black
children than did their black colleagues (Clark, 1964). White
teachers of black children tended to attribute their job
dissatisfactions to factors related to the children and their
parents, whereas black teachers in the same schools were more
critical of teaching conditions, such as overcrowded classrooms
and inadequate supplies (Gottlieb, 1964). McCandless, Roberts,
and Starnes (1972) found that both black and white teachers had
unrealistically high expectations for white students, but not for
black students. One of the major goals of multicultural teacher
education is to make teachers aware of their own biases and to
provide experiences that challenge them so that teachers do not
approach students with discriminatory attitudes.

Children's same-race preference patterns contribute to the
challenge of making racially mixed classrooms truly integrated.
Likewise, the ease with which children absorb prevailing attitudes
often interferes with the development of positive intergroup
attitudes and relationships. A primary goal of multicultural
education is to counteract these trends by challenging students'
assumptions and creating environments that are conducive to
positive intergroup contacts.

In his extensive analysis of the effects of caste on the
educational performance of minority and low status youth in a
number of societies, Ogbu (1978) delineates the many obvious and
subtle ways in which discrimination in schools and employment
negatively affects the quality of education and the academic
engagement of black students. The social reconstuctivist view of
multicultural education addresses this issue in its advocacy for
broader social change.

Children's Responses to Cultural Differences

The terms "culture" and "subculture" refer to the overt and covert expectations of particular social groups. Culture usually refers to one's national group; subculture is a distinct group within a society, and can be defined by national origin, gender, religion, occupation, region, sexual preference, generation, and age. In this country, most people belong to several subcultural groups. The extent to which a person identifies with a particular group is often a matter of individual preference and life history, and frequently shifts across contexts and with developmental and historical changes (Gollnick & Chinn, 1983). Ramirez and Casteneda (1974) describe ways in which individual identities shift and evolve with life experiences and their changing sociohistorical environment.

Ethnic groups, which are the primary focus of this discussion, are defined as people who share a national origin and who, due to their recent arrival, discrimination practiced by the larger society, or by their own choice, remain an identifiable group within the larger cultural environment. In addition to sharing common cultural roots, ethnic groups often have similar physical characteristics and socioeconomic status. Cultural groups that are defined by religion, age, occupation, sexual preference, and other characteristics that are not based on national origin are not considered to be ethnic groups.

The history and current status of the relationship between the national society and a particultar ethnic group are critical to understanding the development of awareness and attitudes of and about its members. If a group has been historically in a position of power and affluence, its members will have values, roles and aspirations that differ considerably from those of a group that has been in a subordinate or oppressed role. Cultural and subcultural expectations, roles, and values influence all aspects of behavior. People outside of a particular culture usually notice concrete manifestations such as language, food, artifacts, music, clothing, and holiday celebrations. However, culture also shapes nuances of social behaviors, such as pace of conversation, nonverbal communications, entry behaviors, acceptable level of conflict, and role expectations. Longstreet (1978) describes many of the subtle ways in which verbal and nonverbal communications, orientation modes, and social value patterns differ across ethnic groups.

Culturally related behaviors are organized and interdependent, and reflect the historical and contemporary economic, social, and political realities of a particular population. Parents seek to inculcate the values and behaviors that are most adaptive to the life circumstances of their children, and children strive, both consciously and unconsciously, to acquire these attributes (Ogbu, 1982). Numerous cross-cultural studies have identified many of these variations in personal and social behavior. These dimensions of cultural differences are summarized by Rotheram and Phinney (1987b) as follows: individual versus group oriented; active versus passive; authoritarian versus egalitarian; expressive versus restrained.

Many cross-cultural studies have embodied a European interpretation of societies and behaviors which is analogous to the Anglocentric orientation in schools discussed in Chapter I. This approach has been criticized from a more pluralistic perspective for presenting biased or inaccurate pictures of different groups. In his critique of European-oriented psychology, Ramirez (1983) discusses how its analytical and compartmentalized approach makes it inadequate for understanding and intervening with people from different cultures. He illustrates how both the process and content of European psychology often leads to an incomplete and a deficit-oriented study and treatment of people from other cultures.

Children's Understanding of Culture

Despite its profound influence on the development of behavior and expectations, and the plethora of cross-cultural studies, very few researchers have examined children's understanding of culture. One exception has been Lambert and Klineberg's study of children's ideas about people of different nationalities (1967). With the rise of the ethnic studies movement, there were also some books that attempted to define ethnicity and to articulate how it affected personal and social development (e.g., Gollnick & Chinn, 1983; Longstreet, 1978), but these writings did not directly address children's understanding of culture.

One reason for the lack of work in this area is the difficulty in designing appropriate measures, because culture is not as concretely visible as race. Furthermore, young children cannot grasp the relationships between societies and subcultures and locations and behaviors. Piaget and Weil (1951) found that children under six could not conceptualize the hierarchical relationships between town, state, and country. Lambert and Klineberg (1967) found that six-year-olds had only a vague notion of what a nation was. Although young children cannot grasp the concept of culture, their social expectations and behaviors are influenced by it from the time they are born (Longstreet, 1978), and they often notice when their culturally specific expectations are violated. Whiting & Whiting's work (1975), in which they compared children's social behaviors across six cultures,

illustrates how culturally related roles and expectations shape
children's social development.

In elementary school, children who are exposed to different
cultural groups begin to form expectations about the behaviors of
other ethnic groups (Rotheram & Phinney, 1987a). An ability to
see conventions as unique to a particular culture, rather than as
universal, develops when children are eight or nine (Carter &
Patterson, 1982). Not until adulthood are people able to see
their own behavior as different from that of other ethnic groups
(Rotheram & Phinney, 1987b). As with social behaviors, children
appear to be aware of language differences and to select
same-language peers as friends, but they do not tend to categorize
their peers by language (Doyle, 1982).

Similar to their early understanding of race, young children
do not see their membership in a particular culture as permanent.
Aboud (1987) found that when non-Eskimo children were dressed in
Eskimo clothing, they assumed that they became Eskimos.

Educational Implications

All cultural variables have implications for children's
reactions to classroom social structures, routines, and
expectations. For example, in an ethnographic comparison of a
Head Start program and a middle class preschool, Lubeck (1985)
describes the differences in the structure and use of time, space,
and materials, and the patterns of interactions. These variations
reflected the differences in the social class and cultures of the
children, and those of the staff at each school. Hale-Benson
(1986) advocates the development of new curricula and teaching
practices that are more compatible with the culture of African-
American children.

Because of its potential effects on children's adaptation to
Western education, cognitive style must be considered. Numerous
studies have used Witkin's dimensions of field independence versus
field dependence to compare it across cultures. As reviewed by
Witkins and Berry (1975) and Bagley (1983), culture and
socialization are related to differences in these dimensions of
cognitive style. In general, females are more field dependent
than males, but these differences vary across cultures. Societies
that stress deference to authority, interpersonal relationship and
conformity tend to have more field dependent members, whereas
groups characterized by independence, individuality, and
competition foster the development of a more field independent
cognitive style. In studies which compared children of recent
immigrants to England or the United States with peers who had
remained in the countries of origin, there is some evidence that,
as children become acculturated to their new settings and attend

schools that emphasize more field independent processes, their cognitive style shifts to become more like that of their new peers (Bagley & Verma, 1983). This line of research typifies the Western-orientation of much cross-cultural research and has been criticized by Ramirez (1983) on several accounts. First, the tests commonly used to measure cognitive style have a European world view bias of valuing field independence over "field sensitivity" (the term used by Ramirez). Second, the Western-style tests only measure a limited range of cognitive functioning. Studies that include observational data, as well as test results, have revealed that Mexican-American children, who commonly are assessed as field dependent, are able to flexibly shift from field dependence to field independence as the situation requires it. While he agrees that there are cross-cultural differences in cognitive styles, Ramirez cautions readers to be aware of the pro-European, field independent bias of many studies of cognitive style.

There are many ways in which schools and conventional teaching practices may clash with children's cognitive and learning styles and social behaviors (Mitchell & Watson, 1980). For instance, in some Native American cultures, children learn more through visual observation and physical manipulation, which are less frequently used by American teachers, who rely on verbal instruction (Rohner, 1965).

Relatively few studies exist which examine specific teaching skills and styles that are related to the success or failure of children from different ethnic backgrounds. Kohut (1980) reviewed the few studies that have been done and concluded that ethnicity of the teacher is not a decisive factor. For example, Kleinfeld (1975) found that, irrespective of background, teachers who were effective with Athabascan Indian and Eskimo students were characterized by being able to create a climate of emotional warmth, to form personalized relationships with the students, and to demand high quality of academic work. A great deal of research remains to be done in this area. One goal of multicultural education is to ensure that all children are taught in ways that are most effective, and that respect and build on their cultural styles and experiences. Mitchell and Watson (1980) make several suggestions about the kinds of information that teachers need to know about the children and families that are in their school in order to facilitate a smooth and productive transition from home to school.

Another goal of multicultural education is to foster children's bicultural or multicultural competencies so they can function in a variety of cultural settings. Ramirez (1983) articulated several dimensions of a contemporary multicultural identity (CMI) which includes abilities to function in more than one culture, a commitment to all of the cultural groups in which

one participates, and an ability to transcend one's group in order
to see it from an outside perspective.   In a study of college
students, he found that the subjects who had attained a
multicultural orientation were more able to assume leadership
roles and to mediate among members of different groups.   Ramirez
and Casteneda (1974) and Ramirez (1983) describe ways in which
teachers can foster bicultural and bicognitive development and a
multicultural orientation.

Children's Responses to Socioeconmic Differences

Socioeconomic status is another less concretely visible
social distinction.   Similar to the effects of culture, children
experience disparities in wealth and resources but do not
understand the reasons for them until adolescence.   Status is
further obscured for children, because it reflects not only
income, but other variables, such as educational background
occupational prestige, place of residence, life-style, and
relative autonomy and power (Gollnick & Chinn, 1983)--attributes
that have little meaning for children.
    There have been many studies of the effects of social class
on different aspects of development.   Low income children often
have been found to be deficient in the specific skills that are
being measured.   These findings have been used as arguments for
implementing various compensatory education programs.   However,
arguing from a more pluralistic orientation, McLoyd (1981) has
pointed out that social class differences are often compounded by
middle-class biases inherent in tasks and assessments.   Thus,
while studies of social class differences may provide some useful
guidance to teachers, they should be read with care and
interpreted with caution.

Children's Understanding of Money and Social Class

Children's understanding of money develops in a series of
definite stages (Edwards, 1986; Furth, 1980).   Preschoolers only
vaguely recognize that money is related to buying and, even when
they recognize the relationship, they often think that the change
that people receive back from shopkeepers is their source of
income.   In their early understanding of mathematical
relationships between goods and money, children often assume that
there has to be a rigid one-to-one correspondence between the
number of coins and the number of articles.   As they gain
experiences with money and related transaction, elementary school

children learn that bills and coins have different values and that goods have specific prices. Children's understanding of the source of money and goods goes through a similar transition, from their early assumptions that goods and money are simply given upon request and available when they are needed, to a comprehension of the chains of transactions of both money and goods.

Leahy (1983) has suggested that children's understanding of social class goes through three stages: peripheral, central, and sociocentric. Early elementary school children are likely to both describe and explain poverty and wealth in observable concrete terms, such as numbers of possessions. When they are around ten years of age, children begin to refer to psychological traits, such as motivation, in their descriptions of people from different circumstances and in their explanations for the unequal distribution of resources. Finally, adolescents are able to see the role of the social structure in the unequal distribution of wealth. As children learn about the sources of economic disparity, they also learn the prevailing attitudes about the value of wealth. Even at young ages, children assume that rich people are happier and more likeable than poor people (Naimar, 1983; Ramsey 1986b). They also learn the prevailing social view that poor people are to blame for their misfortune (Gollnick & Chinn, 1983). While children are not able to grasp the causes of wealth and poverty until adolescence, economic status is internalized into children's career aspirations at an early age (de Lone, 1979).

Education Implications

Despite the heterogeneity of children in all social class groups, teachers often classify children by their socioeconomic backgrounds and base their expectations on that factor (Gollnick & Chinn, 1983). In one study, Rist (1970) observed a kindergarten teacher who divided the children into ability groups by the eighth day of school; the groups corresponded with their social class backgrounds. The fact that these groups keep the same composition through the next two years shows how formative this early assessment was in children's subsequent learning. In an analysis of teacher attitudes and practices in low- and high-income schools, Harvey (1980) found that teachers of low-income children were concerned about their students, but not optimistic about their futures. They discouraged active behavior, used directive teaching techniques, and stressed basic skills. The teacher in the middle-class schools encouraged active and independent learning, emphasized science and art as well as basic skills, and were more positive and optimistic about their students. Using a broad range of sociological and economic data, Bowles and Gintis

(1976) describe how social class distinctions are maintained in public schools, despite their mission to equalize opportunities. Lubeck's (1985) comparision between the Head Start and middle class preschool programs demonstrates how soon this differentiation begins. Mortimore and Mortimore (1986) articulate ways in which the British schools perpetuate social class differences through unequal distribution of resources, teacher attitudes, the examination system, and peer influence. In addition to these factors within schools, disparities in social and economic opportunities also affect the school performance of children from different income groups (Ogbu, 1978).

The ways in which children develop their ideas about money and social class suggest that children notice differences long before they can understand them. The challenge for teachers in the younger grades is to include material that conveys information about the range of affluence in this country, and in the world, and to find developmentally appropriate ways to explain these differences.

Summary

Children are learning about racial, cultural, and socioeconomic differences throughout their childhood. While they do not fully understand the causes and ramifications of these variations until they reach adolescence or adulthood, they are experiencing the implications of these differences in all aspects of their lives. By understanding how awareness and attitudes develop, educators can design more effective multicultural curriculum and teaching strategies. Teachers and administrators also react to these differences in ways which affect children's performance and adjustment in school. Knowledge of the social, cultural, and economic contexts of their children's lives will enable teachers to develop more effective and more suitable teaching practices.

References

Aboud, Frances E. "The Development of Ethnic Self-Identification and Attitudes." Children's Ethnic Socialization. Edited by Jean Phinney and Mary Jan Rotheram. Beverly Hills, CA: Sage Publications, 1987, pp. 32-55.

Aboud, Frances E. "Interest in Ethnic Information: A Cross-Cultural Developmental Study." Journal of Behavioral Science 9 (1977): 134-46.

Aboud Frances E., and Shelagh A. Skerry. "The Development of Ethnic Attitudes: A Critical Review." Journal of Cross-Cultural Psychology 15, 1984, 3-34.

Alejandro-Wright, Marguerite N. "The Child's Conception of Racial Classification: A Socio-Cognitive Developmental Model." Beginnings: The Social and Affective Development of Black Children. Edited by Margaret B. Spencer, Geraldine K. Brookins, and Walter R. Allen. Hillsdale, NJ: Lawrence Erlbaum Associates, 1985, pp. 185-200.

Allport, Gordon W. The Nature of Prejudice. Cambridge, MA: Addison-Wesley, 1954.

Asher, Steven R., Louise C. Singleon, and Angela R. Taylor. "Acceptance versus Friendship: A Longitudinal Study of Racial Integration." Paper presented at the annual meeting of the American Educational Research Association, New York, 1982.

Bagley, Christopher. "Cognitive Styles, Ethnicity, Social Class and Socialization in Cross-Cultural Perspective." Multicultural Childhood. Edited by Christopher Bagley and Gajendra K. Verma. Hampshire, England: Gower Publishing Company, 1983, pp. 3-15.

Bagley, Christopher, and Gajendra K. Verma (Eds.) Multicultural Childhood. Hampshire, England: Gower Publishing Company, 1983.

Bowles, Samuel, and Herbert Gintis. Schooling in Capitalist America: Educational Reform and the Contradictions of Economic Life. New York: Basic Books, 1976.

Brand, Elaine S., Rene A. Ruiz, and Amado M. Padilla. "Ethnic Identification and Preference: A Review." Psychological Bulletin 81 (1974): 860-90.

Carter, D. Bruce, and C. J. Patterson. "Sex Roles as Social Conventions: The Development of Children's Conceptions of Sex-Role Stereotypes." Developmental Psychology 18 (1982): 812-24.

Clark, Audrey, Dennis Hocevar, and Myron H. Dembo. "The Role of Cognitive Development in Children's Explanations and Preferences for Skin Color." Developmental Psychology 16 (1980): 332-39.

Clark, Kenneth B. "Clash of Cultures in the Classroom." Learning Together. Edited by Meyer Weinberg. Chicago: Integrated Education Associates, 1964, pp. 18-25.

Clark, Kenneth B., and Mamie P. Clark. "Racial Identification and Preference in Negro Children. Readings in Social Psychology Edited by Theodore M. Newcomb and Eugene L. Hartley. New York: Holt, Rinehart & Winston, 1947, pp. 169-78.

Cross, William E. "Black Identity; Rediscovering the Distinction between Personal Identity and Reference Group Orientation." Beginnings: The Social and Affective Development of Black Children. Edited by Margaret B. Spencer, Geraldine K. Brookins, and Walter R. Allen. Hillsdale, NJ: Lawrence Erlbaum Associates, 1985, pp. 155-71.

Cross, William E. "A Two Factor Theory of Black Identity: Implications for the Study of Identity Development in Minority Children." Children's Ethnic Socialization. Edited by Jean Phinney and Mary Jane Rotheram. Beverly Hills, CA: Sage Publications, 1987, pp. 117-33.

Davidson, Florence H. "Ability to Respect Persons Compared to Ethnic Prejudice in Childhood." Journal of Personality and Social Psychology 34 (1976): 1256-67.

de Lone, Richard H. Small Future. New York: Harcourt Brace Jovanovich, Inc., 1979.

Doyle, Anna-Beth. "Friends, Acquaintances, and Strangers." Peer Relationships and Social Skills in Childhood. Edited by Kenneth H. Rubin and Hildy S. Ross. New York: Springer-Verlag, 1982.

Edwards, Carolyn Pope. Promoting Social and Moral Development in Young Children: Creative Approaches for the Classroom. New York: Teachers College Press, 1986.

Farrell, Walter C., and James Olson. "Kenneth Clark Revisited: Racial Identification in Light-Skinned and Dark-Skinned Black Children." Paper presented at the annual meeting of the American Educational Research Association, New York, 1982.

Finkelstein, Neal W., and Ron Haskins. "Kindergarten Children Prefer Same-Color Peers." Child Development 54 (1983): 502-508.

Furth, Hans G. The World of Grown-ups: Children's Conceptions of Society. New York: Elsevier, 1980.

Gollnick, Donna M., and Philip C. Chinn. Multicultural Education in a Pluralistic Society. St. Louis: C. V. Mosby, 1983.

Goodman, Mary Ellen. Race Awareness in Young Children. Cambridge, MA: Addison-Wesley, 1952.

Gottlieb, David. "Teaching and Students: The View of Negro and White Teachers." Sociology of Education 27 (1964): 345-353.

Hale-Benson, Janice E. Black Children: Their Roots, Culture, and Learning Styles. Baltimore: Johns Hopkins, 1986.

Harvey, Mary R. "Public School Treatment of Low-Income Children: Education for Passivity." Urban Education 15 (October 1980): 279-323.

Jarrett, Olga, and Lorene Quay. "Cross-Racial Acceptance and Best Friend Choice in Racially Balanced Kindergarten and First-Grade Classrooms." Paper presented at the biennial meeting of the Society for Research in Child Development, Detroit, 1983.

Katz, Phyllis A. "The Acquisition of Racial Attitudes in Children." Towards the Elimination of Racism. New York: Pergamon Press, 1976a, pp. 125-54.

Katz, Phyllis A. "Development of Children's Racial Awareness and
    Intergroup Attitudes." Current Topics in Early Childhood
    Education. Edited by Lilian G. Katz. Norwood, NJ: Ablex,
    1982, pp. 17-54.

Kleinfeld, Judith. "Effective Teachers of Eskimo and Indian
    Students." School Review 83 (1975): 301-44.

Kohlberg, Lawrence. "A Cognitive-Developmental Analysis of
    Children's Sex-Role Concepts and Attitudes." The Development
    of Sex Differences. Edited by Eleanor E. Maccoby. Stanford
    CA: Stanford University Press, 1986, 82-173.

Kohut, Sylvester. "Field Experiences in Preservice Professional
    Studies." Multicultural Teacher Education: Preparing
    Educators to Provide Educational Equity, volume one. Edited
    by H. Prentice Baptiste, Mira L. Baptiste, and Donna M.
    Gollnick. Washington, DC: American Association of Colleges
    for Teacher Education, 1980, pp. 73-93.

Lambert, Wallace E. and Otto Klineberg. Children's View of
    Foreign Peoples. New York: Appleton-Century-Crofts, 1967.

Leahy, Robert L. "The Development of the Conception of Social
    Class." The Child's Construction of Inequality. Edited by
    Robert L. Leahy. New York: Academic Press, 1983, pp.
    79-107.

Longstreet, Wilma S. Aspects of Ethnicity: Understanding
    Differences in Pluralistic Classrooms. New York: Teachers
    College Press, 1978.

Lubeck, Sally. Sandbox Society: Early Education in Black and
    White America. London: The Falmer Press, 1985.

McCandless, Boyd R., Albert Roberts, and Thomas Starnes.
    "Teacher's Marks, Achievement Test Scores, and Aptitude
    Relations with Respect to Social Class, Race, Sex." Journal
    of Educational Psychology 63 (1972): 153-59.

McLoyd, Vonnie C. "Social Class Differences in Sociodramatic
    Play: A Critical Review." Developmental Review 2 (1982): 1
    - 30.

Milner, David. Children and Race. Beverly Hills, CA: Sage
    Publications, 1983.

Mitchell, Edna, and Marilyn Watson. "Personal Cultural
    Orientations and Educational Practices." Multicultural

Teacher Education: Preparing Educators to Provide
Educational Equity, Volume one. Edited by H. Prentice
Baptiste, Mira L. Baptiste and Donna M. Gollnick.
Washington, DC: American Association of Colleges for Teacher
Education, 1980, pp. 154-176.

Mortimore, Peter and Jo Mortimore. "Education and Social Class."
Education and Social Class. Edited by Rick Rogers. London:
The Falmer Press, 1986.

Naimark, Hedwin. "Children's Understanding of Social Class
Differences." Paper presented at the biennial meeting of the
Society for Research in Child Development, Detroit, 1983.

Ogbu, John U. Minority Education and Caste. New York: Academic
Press, 1978.

Ogbu, John U. "Socialization: A Cultural Ecological Approach."
The Social Life of Children in a Changing Society. Edited by
Kathryn M. Borman, Hillsdale, NJ: Lawrence Erlbaum
Associates, 1982.

Patchen, Martin. Black-White Contact in Schools: Its Social and
Academic Effects. West Lafayette, IN: Purdue University
Press, 1982.

Piaget, Jean and Anne-Marie Weil. "The Development in Children of
the Idea of the Homeland and of Relations with Other
Countries." International Social Science Bulletin 3 (1951):
561-78.

Porter, Judith D. R. Black Child, White Child: The Development of
Racial Attitudes. Cambridge, MA: Harvard University Press,
1971.

Ramirez, Manuel III. Psychology of the Americas: Mestizo
Perspectives on Personality and Mental Health. New York:
Academic Press, 1983.

Ramirez, Manuel III, and Alfred Castaneda. Cultural Democracy,
Bicognitive Development, and Education. New York: Academic
Press, 1974.

Ramsey, Patricia G. "Racial and Cultural Categories." Promoting
Social and Moral Development in Young Children: Creative
Approaches for the Classroom. Edited by Carolyn Pope
Edwards. New York: Teachers College Press, 1986a, 78-101.

Ramsey, Patricia G. "Young Children's Understanding of Social
    Class." Paper presented at the annual meeting of the
    American Educational Research Association, San Francisco,
    1986b.

Rex, John. Race and Ethnicity. Milton Keynes, England: Open
    University Press, 1986.

Rist, Ray C. "Student Social Class and Teacher Expectations: The
    Self-Fulfilling Prophecy in Ghetto Education." Harvard
    Educational Review 40 (1970): 411-51.

Rohner, Ronald P. "Factors Influencing the Academic Performance
    of Kwakiutl Children in Canada." Comparative Education
    Review 9 (1965): 331-40.

Rohrer, Georgia K. "Racial and Ethnic Identification and
    Preference in Young Children." Young Children. 32 (1977):
    24-33.

Rosenfield, David & Walter G. Stephan. "Intergroup Relations
    Among Children." Developmental Social Psychology. Edited by
    Sharon S. Brehm, Saul M. Kassin, & Frederick X. Gibbons. New
    York: Oxford University Press, 1981, pp. 271-97.

Rotheram, Mary Jane, and Jean Phinney. "Ethnic Behavior Patterns
    as an Aspect of Identity." Children's Ethnic Socialization:
    Pluralism and Development. Edited by Jean Phinney and Mary
    Jan Rotheram. Beverly Hills, CA: Sage Publications, 1987a,
    pp. 201-18.

Rotheram, Mary Jane, and Jean Phinney. "Introduction:
    Definitions and Perspectives in the Study of Children's
    Ethnic Socialization." Children's Ethnic Socialization:
    Pluralism and Development. Edited by Jean Phinney and Mary
    Jane Rotheram. Beverly Hills, CA: Sage Publications, 1987b,
    pp. 10-28.

St. John, Nancy H. School Desegregation: Outcomes for Children.
    New York: John Wiley & Sons, 1975.

Schofield, Janet W. Black and White in School: Trust, Tension,
    or Tolerance. New York: Praeger, 1982.

Schofield, Janet W. "Complementary and Conflicting Identities:
    Images and Interactions in an Interracial School." The
    Development of Children's Friendships. Edited by Steven R.
    Asher and John M. Gottman. New York: Cambridge University
    Press, 1981, pp. 53-90.

Semaj, Leachim T.   "The Development of Racial-Classification
     Abilities."   Journal of Negro Education 50 (1981):   41-47.

Sigelman, Carol K., and Louise C. Singleton.   "Stigmatization in
     Childhood: A Survey of Developmental Trends and Issues."
     The Dilemmas of Difference: A Multidisciplinary View of
     Stigma.   Edited by Stephen C. Ainlay, Gaylene Becker, and
     Lerita M. Coleman.   New York: Plenum Press, 1986, pp.
     185-208.

Singleton, Louise C., and Steven R. Asher.   "Peer Preferences and
     Social Interactions among Third-Grade Children in an
     Integrated School District." Journal of Educational
     Psychology 69 (1977):   330-36.

Slavin, Richard E.   "Cooperative Learning."   Review of Educational
     Research 50 (1980):   315-42.

Tajfel, Henri.   Human Groups and Social Categories.   New York:
     Cambridge University Press, 1981.

Whiting, Beatrice B., and John W. Whiting.   Children of Six
     Cultures: A Psycho-Cultural Analysis.   Cambridge, MA:
     Harvard University Press, 1975.

Williams, John E., and J. Kenneth Morland.   Race, Color and the
     Young Child.   Chapel Hill, NC: University of North Carolina
     Press, 1976.

Witkin, Herman A., and J. W. Berry.   "Psychological
     Differentiation in Cross-Cultural Perspective."   Journal of
     Cross-Cultural Psychology 6 (1975):   4 - 87.

Bibliography

37. Aboud, Frances E. "The Development of Ethnic
        Self-Identification and Attitudes." Children's Ethnic
        Socialization. Edited by Jean Phinney and Mary Jane
        Rotheram. Beverly Hills, Calif.: Sage Publications,
        1987, pp. 32-55.

        In this chapter, the author reviews studies done since
    1965 on the development of ethnic identity and attitudes
    towards one's own group and other groups. She describes the
    sequence of development and the ways in which children's
    responses differ from adults, and criticizes the methods
    used to measure these variables. The author also
    articulates issues that need more study in each of these
    areas, and concludes with a discussion of the relationship
    between identity and attitudes.

38. Aboud Frances E., and Shelagh A. Skerry. "The Development of
        Ethnic Attitudes: A Critical Review." Journal of
        Cross-Cultural Psychology 15 (1984): 3-34.

        This review of research on the development of ethnic
    attitudes is organized around three issues: the age of
    acquisition of ethnic attitudes, the course of development
    of these attitudes during the childhood years, and the
    psychological factors that contribute to this development.
    In their discussion of the developmental changes, the
    authors describe the different patterns that are evident
    across ethnic groups. They analyze several of the commonly
    used assessment techniques in terms of their contributions
    and limitations, and also comment on the theoretical nature
    of most research in this area. In their analysis of the
    affective, perceptual, and cognitive factors that contribute
    to the development of these attitudes, the authors conclude
    that there are two overlapping sequences occurring during

childhood: a shift from focus on self to a focus on groups, to a focus on individuals, and a sequence of differentiation from affective, to perceptual, to cognitive.

39. Bagley, Christopher. "Cognitive Styles, Ethnicity, Social Class and Socialization in Cross-Cultural Perspective." Multicultural Childhood. Edited by Christopher Bagley and Gajendra K. Verma. Hampshire, England: Gower Publishing Company, 1983, pp. 3-15.

Describes the characteristics associated with field dependence and independence. In a brief review of some of the cross-cultural research, the author compares findings with British, African American, and Caribbean populations. He discusses the possible factors that may contribute to the correlation of field dependence with both traditionalist cultures and low income groups.

40. Bagley, Christopher, and Gajendra K. Verma (Eds.). Multicultural Childhood. Hampshire, England: Gower Publishing Company, 1983.

Part I of this book includes four studies that each contribute to the existing knowledge about the interplay between culture and cognitive style. There are two studies that identify particular factors that are relevant for students undergoing a change in their cultural milieu (e.g. recent immigrants). Another study on Japanese children begins to differentiate some of the educational factors that may contribute to the development of culturally associated cognitive styles. In a study of English children, the relationship between cognitive style and self-esteem is analyzed in terms of its cultural specificity. Part II of the book includes several studies of how members of different cultural groups experience the transition from school to work. The final part of the book is comprised of two studies of differential effects on national social policy on various groups.

41. Bowles, Samuel, and Herbert Gintis. Schooling in Capitalist America: Educational Reform and the Contradictions of Economic Life. New York: Basic Books, 1976.

The authors view the U.S. educational system as a means of supporting the current economic system, rather than as a

potential source of social change. They support their
thesis by showing how educational reform historically has
been tied to changing economic needs and structures, and
demonstrate how schools do not change the degree of
inequality, but simply reproduce it. Their analysis lends
support to the social reconstructivist perspective by
showing that true educational reform cannot occur outside of
the context of profound social and economic changes.

42. Cross, William E. "Black Identity; Rediscovering the
     Distinction between Personal Identity and Reference
     Group Orientation." Beginnings: The Social and
     Affective Development of Black Children. Edited by
     Margaret B. Spencer, Geraldine K. Brookins, and Walter
     R. Allen. Hillsdale, NJ: Lawrence Erlbaum Associates,
     1985, pp. 155-71.

     Cross reviews 161 black identity studies that were
conducted between 1939 and 1977. He articulates the
distinction between assessments of group reference
orientation, in which race or color is an explicit attribute
of the stimulus materials and scoring technique, and
measures of personal identity, which focus on universal
personality elements. He tabulates the number of studies
that fit into each or both categories and then analyzes the
previous conclusions drawn from these studies in light of
this distinction. He concludes that blacks have had a
consistently high self esteem and have had a multifaceted
reference group orientation. The Black Movement in the
later part of this century has not changed the blacks'
personal self-esteem, but has increased the degree of black
reference group orientation. Reference group orientation is
related to value systems, political posture, and likelihood
of joining a collective struggle, but not to personal
self-esteem.

43. Cross, William E. "A Two Factor Theory of Black Identity:
     Implications for the Study of Identity Development in
     Minority Children." Children's Ethnic Socialization.
     Edited by Jean Phinney and Mary Jane Rotheram. Beverly
     Hills, CA: Sage Publications, 1987, pp. 117-33.

     Cross further develops the distinction between
reference group orientation and personal identity in this
chapter, in which he critiques findings of studies that try
to attribute personality changes to increased black
reference group orientation. He points out that in this

country black children are raised with a biracial group
orientation, whereas white children are more likely to grow
up with a monoracial world view.

44. de Lone, Richard H. _Small Futures: Children, Inequality,
    and the Limits of Liberal Reform._ New York: Harcourt
    Brace Jovanovich, Inc., 1979.

    The major theme of this book is that social change
    cannot be effected by social reforms such as educational
    improvement, but requires that economic and social
    structures be changed to provide more ample futures for
    children. The author articulates how the unequal
    distribution of wealth ensures the inequality of children's
    opportunities, despite efforts at social reform. He
    critiques current theories of child development that accept
    and rationalize this inequality, and advocates a situational
    theory of child development that studies development in the
    context of society, class, and history. Of particular
    relevance to educators is his account of how chidren develop
    theories of social reality that reflect the lives of adults
    with whom they identify. The author concludes with
    strategies to create more egalitarian family structures.

45. Edwards, Carolyn Pope. _Promoting Social and Moral
    Development in Young Children: Creative Approaches for
    the Classroom._ New York: Teachers College Press,
    1986.

    Describes the early development of children's
    understanding about their social environment, specifically
    age groups, gender and sex-roles, race, culture, family,
    friends, social institutions (including the economic system
    and occupations), rules, and authority. For each area,
    activities called "thinking games" are included to help
    teachers design activities to both elicit how children think
    about these aspects of their environment and to broaden
    children's awareness of different social phenomena.

46. Furth, Hans G. _The World of Grown-ups: Children's
    Conceptions of Society._ New York: Elsevier, 1980.

    This is a description of a major research project in
    which the author interviewed 195 British children, ages 5 -
    11, about their understanding of communities, societies,
    money, stores, schools, bus systems, and government. The

author found that children appeared to go through four
stages of societal understanding from personalistic
interpretations of social institutions to a more systematic
framework. Transcripts of the children's responses are
included to provide the reader with specific examples of how
children perceive and process social information during the
childhood years.

47. Gay, Geneva and Willie L. Baber (Eds.). Expressively Black:
    The Cultural Basis of Ethnic Identity. New York:
    Praeger, 1987.

    This edited volume offers a multidisciplinary
perspective on expressiveness in all dimensions of life that
is a characteristic feature of Afro-American culture. The
initial chapters include descriptions of the role of black
expressiveness in kinship patterns and identity development.
Subsequent chapters illustrate how this dynamic emerges in
Afro-American music, art, drama, poetry, film, and
leadership style. The final chapters discuss the
communicative spirit that prevails in the black community
and the cultural continuity between African and
Afro-American experiences. The book is rich in observations
and personal accounts that enable the reader to both
experience the flavor of black expressiveness and appreciate
its role in Afro-American culture.

48. Gollnick, Donna M., and Philip C. Chinn. Multicultural
    Education in a Pluralistic Society. St. Louis: C. V.
    Mosby, 1983.

    The authors discuss several dimensions of plurality,
including ethnicity, religion, language, socioeconomic
status, sex, age, and exceptionality. They devote a chapter
to each one and describe the history, social context, and
effects of each aspect on social relationships,
opportunities, and personal development. Implications for
educational practices related to each area are also
discussed. The concluding chapter is a description of
general strategies for multicultural education.

49. Hale-Benson, Janice E. Black Children: Their Roots,
    Culture, and Learning Styles. Baltimore: Johns
    Hopkins, 1986.

    Drawing on numerous anthropological, sociological,
psychological, and historical studies (primarily done from

the 1950s through the 1970s), the author describes how the African heritage has shaped the Afro-American culture. She contrasts the distinctive characteristics of black children's cognitive styles, family experiences, and play behaviors with the Anglo-oriented behavioral expectations that typify American schools. Her thesis is that this poor match between schools and children accounts for the lower educational performances of black children. She advocates the development of pedagogical practices and curricula that are more compatible with the learning styles of Afro-American children. Her analysis of Afro-American culture and her educational recommendations created a considerable amount of controversy when the book was first published in 1982. Many readers thought that she ignored the cultural variety within the black community and was advocating separate and possibly inferior schools for black children. In the more recent edition, she addresses some of the criticisms, and emphasizes that black children should not be isolated from the larger society.

50. Harvey, Mary R. "Public School Treatment of Low-Income Children: Education for Passivity." Urban Education 15 (October 1980): 279-323.

Using extensive teacher interviews and classroom observations, Harvey compares the teacher attitudes and classroom practices in eight second grades, half of which were in low-income schools and half were in high-income areas. The findings suggest that teachers of low-income children are concerned about their students, but not optimistic about their futures. They discourage active behavior, use more directive techniques, and stress basic skills. In contrast, teachers in the more affluent schools more positively describe their students, encourage independent and active learning, and include a broader range of curricula. The author discusses the long-range educational implications of these differences.

51. Katz, Phyllis A. "The Acquisition of Racial Attitudes in Children." Towards the Elimination of Racism. New York: Pergamon Press, 1976, pp. 125-54.

The author reviews and synthesizes the research on the development of racial attitudes conducted prior to 1976. She delineates and compares some of the environmental factors that influence the course of racial attitude development, including reinforcement, direct instruction, and child-rearing styles, and the psychological factors,

such as perception, cognition, and personality. Racial
attitude acquisition is compared with the development of
other attitudes such as sex-roles and proposes a sequence of
eight overlapping stages which span the preschool and
elementary years.

52. Katz, Phyllis A. "Development of Children's Racial
       Awareness and Intergroup Attitudes." Current Topics in
       Early Childhood Education. Edited by Lilian G. Katz.
       Norwood, NJ: Ablex, 1982, pp. 17-54.

       This chapter is a review of theories and research about
the course of the development of children's racial
attitudes. Based on research prior to 1982, it includes a
discussion of the developmental forerunners of racial
attitudes and a critique of commonly used measurements of
racial awareness. There is a review and synthesis of the
environmental and psychological mechanisms that underlie the
development of racial attitudes and a comparison between
this development and that of other attitudes.

53. Katz, Phyllis A. (Ed.). Towards the Elimination of Racism.
       New York: Pergamon Press, 1976.

       This book contains 11 essays that address several major
issues, theories, and research findings on racial attitude
development and change. The authors represent a number of
fields, including psychology, sociology, communications, and
government. The book is divided into three sections. The
first part includes three essays that summarize several
theoretical viewpoints about the factors that account for
the acquisition and maintenance of negative racial
attitudes. In the second section, research on the
modification of individual racial attitudes and behavior in
children and adults is reported. The final section focuses
on institutional racism, such as employment patterns and
resistance to legal reform.

54. Leahy, Robert L. "The Development of the Conception of
       Social Class." The Child's Construction of Inequality.
       Edited by Robert L. Leahy. New York: Academic Press,
       1983, pp. 79-107.

       The author first reviews several theories and previous
research on the concept of social class and its development.
He then proposes a cognitive-developmental theory of the
acquisition of the conceptions of social class that reflects

the qualitative changes observed by Piaget in his work on children's development of knowledge. A study of 720 children from the ages of six through adolescence is used to illustrate how children's concepts of social class progress through qualitatively different stages. His inquiries include children's concepts of wealth and poverty, explanations for inequality, and ideas about individual mobility and social change. He describes the levels of class conceptions and uses quotes from the interview transcripts to illustrate how children are thinking about social class.

55. Longstreet, Wilma S. Aspects of Ethnicity: Understanding Differences in Pluralistic Classrooms. New York: Teachers College Press, 1978.

The author discusses the subtle cultural differences and defines ethnicity as "that portion of cultural development that occurs before the individual is in complete command of his or her abstract intellectual powers and that is formed primarily through the individual's early contacts with family, neighbors, friends, teachers, and others..." She identifies and discusses five aspects of ethnicity: verbal communication, nonverbal communication, orientation modes, social value patterns, and intellectual modes that have implications for cross-cultural communication and teaching diverse populations. Methods of learning about these behavioral nuances are described in detail and illustrated with anecdotes and examples.

56. Lubeck, Sally. Sandbox Society: Early Education in Black and White America. London: The Falmer Press, 1985.

In this ethnographic study, the author compares two pre-school classrooms: one is a Head Start program for low-income children and the other one is a middle-class program. Working as a participant observer over a period of a few months, the author observed and recorded the ways in which the teachers structured the programs, and the actions of the children. She analyzed the observations by comparing the two programs on the following dimensions: allocations of time, use of space, structure and use of activities and materials, and patterns of teacher-child interactions. In her analysis, she concluded that the cultures of the two communities were transmitted in many subtle ways through teaching practices.

57. Milner, David. Children and Race. Beverly Hills, CA: Sage
        Publications, 1983.

        This book begins with two chapters on the historical
     background about the popular concepts and attitudes related
     to race and the ways in which psychologists have studied
     prejudice. The next two chapters discuss psychological and
     social factors that contribute to the development of racial
     attitudes. The author describes the ways in which
     prejudices and stereotypes are evident in children's
     literature and the media. The fourth chapter is a review of
     the research that has been done on the development of racial
     attitudes. The next chapter focuses on the effects of
     racism on the development of black children. The final two
     chapters discuss the educational implications of widely held
     racist views, and ways in which education could be more
     equitable.

58. Ogbu, John U. Minority Education and Caste. New York:
        Academic Press, 1978.

        In this analysis of blacks' educational performance,
     Ogbu attributes their lack of success to the caste system in
     this country, which relegates blacks to a subordinate status
     in this society. He describes how this system influences
     both the quality of education available to blacks and their
     performance in schools as an adaptation to that system. He
     discusses the educational experiences of other groups in the
     United States and in other countries which are also caste
     like minorities, although not necessarily racially distinct
     from the more privileged members of the society. He
     concludes by discussing the policy implications of his
     interpretation of black school performance.

59. Ogbu, John U. "Socialization: A Cultural Ecological
        Approach." The Social Life of Children in a Changing
        Society. Edited by Kathryn M. Borman, Hillsdale, NJ:
        Lawrence Erlbaum Associates, 1982.

        This work criticizes many cross-cultural studies for
     assuming a causal relationship between childrearing
     techniques and outcomes, often concluding that the parenting
     skills of the poor are deficient to teach children how to
     cope with middle-class life. The author advocates that
     childrearing styles be analyzed in the context of the
     social, political, and economic realities of each group and

the competencies that are needed to function as adult members of that society or social group. He illustrates this causal relationship by describing the social and economic structure of other societies and oppressed groups within the United States society, and the ways in which childrearing values and techniques are geared to the competencies demanded of adults in these groups.

60. Patchen, Martin. Black-White Contact in Schools: Its Social and Academic Effects. West Lafayette, IN: Purdue University Press, 1982.

The author reports findings from a study of 11 recently desegregated high schools in which multiple assessments of interracial relations were used to examine the personal and environmental factors that were related to positive or negative cross-group relationships. Besides presenting summative profiles of intergroup contacts, the author also includes examples from interviews that show how attitudes and relationships develop. The second part of the book examines the effects of desegregation on the academic achievements of both black and white students.

61. Phinney, Jean S., and Mary Jane Rotheram. Children's Ethnic Socialization: Pluralism and Development. Beverly Hills, CA: Sage Publications, 1987.

This edited volume has 15 essays that cover several aspects of children's ethnic socialization, including the individual variables of cognition, identification, language, and behavior and the enviromental ones of minority status and sociohistorical context. Taken together, the essays address issues germane to young children, school-aged children, and adolescents. The editors conclude that ethnic group differences, the sociocultural context of these differences, the status of one's group, and the developmental stages are all critical elements in the ethnic socialization of children.

62. Ramirez, Manuel III. Psychology of the Americas: Mestizo Perspectives on Personality and Mental Health. New York: Academic Press, 1983.

In this critique of European psychology, Ramirez contrasts the origins, roles, and assumptions of European and Mestizo psychologies and discusses how relying only on

European psychology limits our understanding of non-European
people and leads to a deficit-orientation in the study of
them. The author describes the philosophical, social
science, and theoretical foundations of Mestizo Psychology,
which has a phenomenalist orientation, viewing people in a
more holistic way and in the context of their cultural,
social, historical, and economic environments. He proposes
models of research and mental health treatment that are
based on a synthesis of European and Mestizo psychologies
which considers people in the context of their cultural and
sociohistorical environment.

63. Rex, John. Race and Ethnicity. Milton Keynes, England:
        Open University Press, 1986.

        As a sociologist, the author clarifies the concepts of
race and ethnicity and how they relate to each other and
with class and status differences. The relationships
between ethnic and racial groups in both colonial societies
and contemporary urban societies are discussed and compared
between the United States and Britain. The author describes
racist thinking and racist institutions in a number of
societies and discusses ways in which societies could become
multicultural.

64. Rogers, Rick. Education and Social Class. London: The
        Falmer Press, 1986.

        This edited volume is the product of a conference held
in Cambridge, England in 1983 on education and social class.
The chapters examine many aspects of the English educational
system that contribute to the gap between social classes and
between British and non-British born students. The factors
that contribute to the disparity in school achievement,
examination results, and employment prospects are discussed
in depth, and possible directions for change are offered.
Issues related to the development of a comprehensive school
system (instead of the traditional two-tiered system) and
the extensive use of private education on the part of the
more affluent citizens are emphasized throughout the book.

65. Rosenfield, David, and Walter G. Stephan. "Intergroup
        Relations Among Children." Developmental Social
        Psychology. Edited by Sharon S. Brehm, Saul M. Kassin,
        & Frederick X. Gibbons. New York: Oxford University
        Press, 1981, pp. 271-97.

In this chapter, the authors review the cognitive, affective, and behavioral components of racial attitudes, and present findings from a study on the effects of desegregation on elementary children's self-esteem and on their racial attitudes and contact patterns. They also include findings from several studies that have identified factors that appear to contribute to more positive intergroup relations. These factors include school and classroom structures that encourage positive, cooperative intergroup contact; an educational climate that is conducive to interethnic contact; community and family support for integration; and individuals' capabilities to form positive interpersonal relationships.

66. Rotheram, Mary Jane, and Jean Phinney. "Ethnic Behavior Patterns as an Aspect of Identity." Children's Ethnic Socialization: Pluralism and Development. Edited by Jean Phinney and Mary Jan Rotheram. Beverly Hills, Calif: Sage Publications, 1987a, pp. 201-18.

This includes a review of research on cross-cultural differences found along the following dimensions: group versus individual orientation, active versus passive coping styles, attitudes toward authority, expressive versus restrained. The authors describe a method of using videotaped interactions between children of different ethnic groups to assess children's awareness of culturally specific behavior patterns, and the extent to which they identify with their own or other ethnic groups.

67. Rotheram, Mary Jane, and Jean Phinney. "Introduction: Definitions and Perspectives in the Study of Children's Ethnic Socialization." Children's Ethnic Socialization: Pluralism and Development. Edited by Jean Phinney and Mary Jane Rotheram. Beverly Hills, CA: Sage Publications, 1987b, pp. 10-28.

This chapter provides an overview of the theories and research in several areas of young children's socialization, including identity, attitudes about one's own and other groups, and behavior patterns. There is also a brief discussion of the previous research and the samples, methods, and perspectives reflected in these studies.

68. Schofield, Janet W. Black and White in School: Trust, Tension, or Tolerance. New York: Praeger, 1982.

As a report of a three-year longitudinal ethnographic study of a recently opened desegregated middle school, this volume describes the responses of students, teachers, and administrators to a racially mixed environment. Using extensive observations and interviews, the author describes the ways in which teachers unconsciously resegregated students, and mechanisms which students used to avoid cross-race contact and relationship. The interaction of race and gender differences is discussed. In the description of the changes in cross-race behaviors and relationships that occurred during the three years of the study, the author expresses cautious optimism that desegregation can potentially facilitate cross-race understanding and respect.

69. Schofield, Janet W. "Complementary and Conflicting Identities: Images and Interactions in an Interracial School." The Development of Children's Friendships. Edited by Steven R. Asher and John M. Gottman. New York: Cambridge University Press, 1981, pp. 53-90.

Using the ethnographic data described above, the author discusses cross-racial perceptions of both black and white students, and the identity and behavior factors that inhibit the development of strong cross-race friendships. The chapter includes several quotations from students and a discussion of the educational and social implications of these patterns.

70. Sigelman, Carol K., and Louise C. Singleton. "Stigmatization in Childhood: A Survey of Developmental Trends and Issues." The Dilemmas of Difference: A Multidisciplinary View of Stigma. Edited by Stephen C. Ainlay, Gaylene Becker, and Lerita M. Coleman. New York: Plenum Press, 1986, pp. 185-208.

The authors begin by comparing the following three theoretical perspectives on the development of stereotyping and prejudice: psychoanalytic, cognitive-developmental, and social learning. Using all three theories, they trace the perceptual, cognitive, affective, and behavioral development of prejudice from infancy through childhood, and summarize research findings in the areas of racial prejudice and stigmatization of physical disabilities.

71. Spencer, Margaret B., Geraldine K. Brookins, and Walter R. Allen (Eds.). Beginnings: The Social and Affective Development of Black Children. Hillsdale, NJ: Lawrence Erlbaum, 1985.

This volume differs from the vast majority of studies of ethnic groups because it contains studies of black children that were conceptualized and conducted from the perspective of the social ecology of the black experience, rather than from a white middle class perspective. This edited volume contains 17 essays on topics related to the development of black children. The first part focuses on the traditional treatment of blacks in research studies, and on the social context variables that might have a differential impact on black as opposed to white children. The second section consists of several research reports and reviews that articulate black-specific patterns in areas such as sociodramatic play, test performance, teacher-child relationhships, and coping strategies. The next section has five essays on cognitive, personality, and social factors in the development of black children's identities. In the fourth part there are three chapters on black families. The final section is a summary of the major points raised in this volume, and implications for research and social policy.

72. Tajfel, Henri. Human Groups and Social Categories. New York: Cambridge University Press, 1981.

As a social psychologist, the author examines the research in cross-group perceptions, attitudes, and behavior that has been done in Europe and the United States. He emphasizes the need to examine the interplay between individual psychology and relationships with the dynamics of the larger social context. The book includes many descriptions of studies in which the author examined several facets of prejudice in both children and adults from his perspective. The three major areas of investigation are the role of perceptual judgement in creating and maintaining social stereotypes, the effects of being an insider or an outsider, and the intergroup conflict. The studies of children include several on the development of ethnocentrism and understanding different countries.

73. Williams, John E., and J. Kenneth Morland. Race, Color and the Young Child. Chapel Hill, NC: University of North Carolina Press, 1976.

The authors begin this book with a discussion of the
way racial differences have been treated in this country in
laws, religion, literature, and the social sciences. They
then discuss many studies that they have done during the
pervious 15 years in which they examine the development and
modifications of racial attitudes, with a particular
emphasis on the roles of symbolic and biological use of
color. In their reports, the authors discuss numerous
instruments that have been used to measure color attitudes
and racial attitudes, acceptance, preference, and
classification. They also discuss the relationships among
these processes, and integrate them into a theoretical model
of the development of racial bias in young children. With a
strong environmental emphasis, they articulate the ways in
which biases are learned from possible initial preferences
for lightness, general cultural influences, and specific
attitudes of their family and community.

CHAPTER III

MULTICULTURAL PROGRAMS, CURRICULA, AND STRATEGIES

Leslie R. Williams

The evolution of multicultural educational programs, curricula and teaching strategies for young children (ages three to twelve) has paralleled and reflected the broader social, political and educational movements within our society discussed in Chapter I of this source book. As the awareness and sensitivity of educators, curriculum designers, materials developers, and community advocates toward issues of cultural diversity has increased, interest in incorporation of multicultural approaches to educational settings has grown. This interest has shown itself differently and with varying rates of progress in different regions of the country. In many cases it has received its impetus from the swelling numbers of "culturally different" children entering the public schools, and from the observed depressed academic performances of many of those children. Concerned educators in the late 1960s began to seek alternative ways to reach children who did not appear responsive to the schools' traditional instructional practices.

Prior to that period, there had been programs and curricula that focused on intergroup education and ethnic studies (e.g. Epstein, 1968; Grambs, 1968; Taba, Brady and Robinson, 1952). The purpose of these efforts appeared to be promoting positive interactions among racial and ethnic groups, and broadening students' understanding of the contributions of various groups to the United States. Most of them did not explicitly connect such study with heightening academic performance.

As President Johnson's "War on Poverty" was launched in 1965, however, the provision of equal educational opportunity assumed a prominent position in public discourse. Some program developers reoriented their efforts toward remediation of the low academic performance of many "disadvantaged" children. These educators

based their work on the premise that the children had learning
deficits that were environmentally caused (Gray, Klaus, Miller,
and Forrester, 1966; Bereiter and Engelmann, 1966). It was not
long before this "deficit model" for educational intervention was
called into question. Baratz and Baratz (1970) and Valentine   .
(1971), among others, posited that "cultural difference" rather
than deficit was the reason for depressed academic performance.
The implication of this formulation was that school programs and
curricula needed to be restructured to meet the child, rather than
the child changed to meet the demands of the school.

Growth in the popularity of the cultural difference
hypothesis lent support to continuing activity in the ethnic
studies movement and to the introduction of multicultural
education in the mid-1970s. Programs, curricula, and teaching
strategies developed during that period often articulated
improvement of performance in school-related skills as their major
goal. The focus of the work remained on children who were
identified as culturally different from the mainstream population.

As the decade progressed, though, some of the older goals
(that is, promotion of positive interaction among various groups
and broadening understanding of the contributions of all the
groups making up a society to the whole) reasserted themselves and
blended with the focus on academic performance. At the present
time, existing educational materials that designate themselves as
"multicultural" incorporate a range of goals arising from this
history.

The goals behind development of similar programs, curricula,
and teaching strategies in other parts of the English-speaking
world has in many instances followed a path similar to that of the
United States. Williams (1979) has noted that in Great Britain,
the movement toward multicultural education can be seen to have
assumed at least three forms: (1) the "technicist" view, a
compensatory approach intended as an avenue to heightened
performance for culturally different children who were showing
poor self concept; (2) the "moral" view, an approach seen as
suitable for all children for improving self-understanding and, by
extension, understanding of others in ways that will eventually
encourage cooperation among groups and diminish racial and
cultural discrimination; and (3) the "sociopolitical" view, in
which all cultural groups are seen as equal inheritors of
political power, and the inherent domination of minorities by the
majority will cease. The first two views have frequently led to
the design of self-contained curricula or learning experiences,
often presented separately from other areas of learning. The
third view, in contrast, implies permeation of the total
curriculum with a multicultural orientation, so that the student
remains aware of multiple perspectives on any subject.

As previously noted in Chapter I, Sleeter and Grant (1987) have recently advanced a more refined categorization of program orientations. They discern five approaches to program designs, curricula, and strategies that characterize themselves as multicultural, according to underlying purposes and goals: (1) education of the culturally different child (much like the compensatory view above), intended for minority students who are not presently achieving at a high level; (2) single group studies (formerly called "ethnic studies" by Grant and Sleeter), which may be intended for all students or ethnic minorities only, and which treat ethnic groups as distinct entities in separate curricular segments; (3) human relations, focusing on intergroup cooperation for all children, as in Williams' moral view; (4) multicultural education, also similar to the moral view in that it is designed for all children, emphasizes the positive, adaptive value of cultural pluralism, and encourages children's competence in more than one cultural system; and, finally, (5) education that is multicultural and social reconstructionist, a more fully articulated orientation toward change of the deep structures of society that foster unequal relationships among distinct groups. The fifth is the most far-reaching of the approaches; and like the fourth, implies infusion of a multicultural perspective throughout the entire curriculum. The first three formulations, on the other hand, are more likely to take the form of self-contained or "add-on" curricular activities.

It should be noted that in educational resources representing each or combinations of these approaches, there is variation in the terminology used to describe the orientation of the work. The range of designations (multicultural, multiracial, multiethnic, etc.) discussed in Chapter I, with their particular connotations, does appear in the curricular writings, just as it does in the works on policy.

Grant and Sleeter (1984) report that from 1974 to 1984, no clear progression from one to another was evident in the appearance of the five approaches they identified. Recent review by the authors of this source book of conference presentations, and publications from 1984 through 1987, however, indicate that there may be a shift away from education of the culturally different, single group studies, and human relations works, toward multicultural education celebrating cultural pluralism. Resources based on the concept of "education that is multicultural" are still relatively scarce.

This chapter reviews teachers' guides, manuals, books, and other resources published over the last twelve years for early childhood and elementary school settings that focus on the implementation of multicultural approaches fostering cultural pluralism. Works primarily oriented both toward the positive, adaptive value of cultural pluralism and its potential for the creation of social change have been included. (Some resources do contain elements of the three other approaches as well.) Assessment of the suitability of these resources for use in a particular classroom or district is contingent upon an understanding of the range of possibilities that the materials represent. Each resource can be examined not only according to its purposes, but in light of its relationship to other issues and dilemmas inherent in multicultural education today, and in relationship to the overall dimensions of program or curriculum design.

Issues and Dilemmas

Types of Multicultural Materials

The literature on multicultural education refers to programs, curricula, and teaching strategies in what may appear to be an interchangeable manner. There are, however, some conventional definitions that are helpful in sorting out the intent behind the descriptions.

Programs. Use of the term "program" generally implies a fully articulated approach, covering the activities of the classroom and often other components, such as parent participation and staff development, as well. Programs usually include some form of plan for implementation of the approach. Because of the articulation involved, some programs may be considered models. The elements that go into a complete program design or model are discussed in a following section of this chapter.

Curricula. A "curriculum" may refer broadly to the processes used to plan, implement, and evaluate learning activities, or cumulatively, to encompass all the educational activities undertaken in a classroom. More narrowly, curriculum may refer to one stream of those activities (often representing a particular subject such as math, or language arts), which is presented in combination with other streams. Some authors use "curriculum" in a very limited fashion to mean only the content (particular concepts or skills), or only the materials that the children use (books, manipulatives, or workbooks).

Strategies. "Teaching strategies" usually refers to procedures or approaches taken to carry out educational activities. Rather than what is being undertaken, strategies are how the activities are conducted. Strategies may be suggested independently of or in conjunction with specific curriculum materials.

Classroom Materials. In addition to the three types of
resources noted above intended for the teacher's use, there are
now a number of multiculturally oriented classroom or learning
materials designed for the children's direct use. Certain of
these materials are informative enough to provide additional
resources for teachers, as well.

The concept of approaches or orientations to multicultural
education described by Grant and Sleeter (1987) implies the use of
strategies expressive of a particular orientation, just as it
implies use of educational activities and classroom materials that
are congruent with the overall purpose of the approach. Any of
the five approaches may appear in the form of a program, a
curriculum, or a work primarily emphasizing teaching strategies.

Definition of Culture

Aside from basic definitions of the type of resource each
publication represents, there are other issues to consider in
review of available programs and curricula. One is the authors'
understanding of what constitutes "culture." Like definitions of
curriculum, delineation of the elements of culture may run the
gamut from broad processes encompassing both a group's past (its
heritage and tradition) and that group's present living
circumstances (its responses to the requirements of living today),
to narrow conceptualizations of culture as a fixed set of customs
or "folkways." It is the position of the authors of this source
book that the former view of culture as an inclusive and dynamic
expression of life is the more accurate and useful construct.

Materials and resources that draw upon culture as a process
in understanding human experience generally can be adapted
effectively for whatever cultural groups are represented in a
classroom. In contrast, resources which view culture only in
terms of its specific expression for a particular group may be
found to be less versatile, with content requiring total
reconstruction in order to address any other cultural group.
Moreover, resources relying on such a high degree of specificity
in content may be especially prey to stereotypic representations,
as intragroup variation is obscured. Process approaches to the
definition of culture, on the other hand, highlight the
constructive tension between the characteristics of individuals
and group tendencies, revealing culture as a continuous
construction of mind and spirit.

Linguistic and Other Variations

Another issue in multicultural educational materials is the degree of attention paid to linguistic and other variations as aspects of cultural diversity (see Chapter I). While multicultural programs are not necessarily bilingual in instructional practice, and bilingual programs may or may not be multicultural in orientation, the two elements cannot logically be divorced from one another. Language is one of the expressions of culture, and the deep structures of a culture determine when, where, and with whom particular language variations may be employed. In the United States at the present time, however, bilingual education and multicultural education have differing political connotations according to the degree to which the retention of languages other than English has highlighted both the separateness of particular groups and their unequal opportunity in the society in which they are embedded. While this source book has not reviewed materials that are exclusively bilingual in orientation, a number of the programs and curricula in the annotated bibliography include or allude to bilingual options. In a similar manner, materials have been included that address racism, sexism, ageism, or perceptions of handicapping conditions as reflections of social structures requiring change.

Basis for Selecting Multicultural Resources

Use of a multicultural perspective requires either that the programs, curricula, and/or strategies chosen be complementary to existing practice (thus refining ongoing work), or that they serve as vehicles for innovation and change. In either case, the articulation and coherence of the materials and methods selected, and the ways those will impact upon what Sarason (1982) calls the "internal regularities" of the classroom, must be examined. This can be done through review of the elements of program or curriculum design, and examination of individual resources in relation to those dimensions.

Dimensions of Program/Curriculum Design

Philosophy and Population to be Served

The point of departure in sound educational design is commonly conceived as either the philosophy underlying the program (the purposes of the effort) or description of the population to

be served. The two elements are in fact interdependent. The
philosophy or overall orientation will permeate the entire work,
as has been previously discussed, and the way the population to be
served is viewed and defined will be strongly influenced by that
philosophy.

The converse is also true. The view of the child's normal,
developmental course that is accepted by materials developers, the
bodies of theory drawn upon, and the results of research
integrated into conceptualizations of child development and
learning are powerful influences in their turn on the definition
of an underlying philosophy. These considerations do not replace
the sociopolitical consciousness discussed earlier. Rather they
tend to fuel that awareness with empirical evidence to support a
chosen direction. Thus, the importance of acquaintance with the
body of child development literature examining children's
perceptions of race, culture, and class can also be clearly seen.
(See Chapter II for a discussion of that literature.)

Implications, Goals and Objectives

From both the underlying philosophy and the population
description are derived implications for practice. The
implications are the guidelines for action which shape the
arrangement of furniture and materials in the classroom, and the
use of time (schedules). The implications also provide guidance,
along with the philosophy and the population description, to the
further specification of instructional goals and objectives.
Clearly these must represent connections and continuity with the
underlying philosophy and overall purpose of the work, so that the
program or curriculum remains internally coherent. The degree of
specificity used in the statement of goals and objectives, and
whether they are targeted toward children's attitudes and
performance, or procedures for teachers, will vary according to
the implicatons that have been drawn.

Activities, Strategies and Materials

With the establishment of goals and objectives, learning
activities, teaching strategies and classroom materials for the
children's use can be designed. Each of these is properly the
reflection of the deeper structures explained above, which are
foundational to the total program or curriculum. The
effectiveness and the integrity of each depends on how well it
fits within the total system of which it is a part. When
activities, strategies, or materials are selected and integrated
into the multicultural perspective being used, they must be

carefully assessed to determine their appropriateness within the overall purposes of the program.

Assessment and Evaluation

Finally, a sound program or curriculum design will include an assessment or evaluation component. Two types of evaluation are important: first, the assessment of the degree of implementation of the multicultural approach in the classroom; and second, assessment of the impact of the implemented approach on children, teachers, and, as appropriate to the overall design, on parents.

Williams and Cruikshank (1981) have pointed out that while many programs and curricula have been evaluated for impact, few evaluators have first assessed the degree of implementation of the approach. The importance of an implementation evaluation cannot be overstressed, as otherwise it is difficult to determine with any degree of accuracy to what the effects observed are due. Use of checklists of prominent program features that one would expect to observe in a classroom implementing a multicultural approach, observation of teaching strategies and of patterns in children's use of materials, recording of the children's spontaneous comments, and interviews to gather the perceptions of children, teachers, administrators, and parents, are all useful devices for assessment of degree of implementation.

Impact evaluations may be formative or summative in nature (Bloom, Hastings, and Madaus, 1971). Formative evaluations are used throughout the year to feed information back into the ongoing refinement of the program or curriculum. The same sorts of devices used for assessment of implementation may also prove useful as formative evaluations of impact. How completely the children are able to carry out the activities, the use they make of the multicultural learning materials, and the particular ways in which they respond to the teaching strategies are all important indicators that can lead to steady improvement of practice.

Summative evaluations compare the performance of children at the beginning of the year (or at the end of the preceding year) with their performance at the close of the current school term. Standardized tests of acquisition of skills and knowledge, such as language proficiency measures and tests of reading and math skills, are commonly used to determine children's overall progress. A dilemma associated with summative evaluation is that usually the content of the standardized tests does not reflect the goals of a multicultural approach to education, and, therefore, the true effects of the program cannot be assessed in that manner. What may be indicated through summative evaluation is that the use of a multicultural approach to education can heighten performance across curriculum areas. The scores of children before and after

the introduction of the multicultural approach would need to be
compared in order to draw such a conclusion.

Fully articulated program or curriculum designs contain
provisions and offer guidance for evaluation in at least one of
the capacities discussed above. The availability of an evaluation
procedure lends power and persuasiveness to the adoption of a
multicultural approach, and evidence of efficacy is always useful
in the creation of change.

Research on Multicultural Programs
Curricula, and Strategies

While some of the materials annotated below do contain
suggestions for program or curriculum evaluation, virtually
nothing has been published at present that utilizes those
suggestions in formal research on implementation or impact of
particular multicultural programs or curricula. Sleeter and Grant
(1987) note the absence of research on multicultural education,
and remark that authors in the area have had to continue to rely
on studies drawn from other sources (such as child development
studies and anthropological works). The new wave of classroom
investigations appearing in early childhood and elementary school
research (e.g., Gelfand, 1988; Yinger, 1980; Yonemura, 1986), that
describe what actually occurs in teaching/learning situations or
examine relationships between learning contexts and student
outcomes, has apparently not yet influenced multicultural
educators.

One exception to this statement has been a few studies that
examined the effects of particular teaching strategies on student
behaviors, such as use of cross-cultural peer groupings to foster
cooperative learning or to reduce overt expressions of prejudice
(Gimmestad and De Chiara, 1982; Slavin, 1980). While the effects
of such strategies were positive in the short term, no information
is available on long term retention of the attitudes and skills
acquired.

Sleeter and Grant further suggest that the gap in research
may be due in part to the fact that multicultural education itself
has never been targeted for federal funding. What work has been
done under federal sponsorship has been subsidized by such areas
as ethnic studies, bilingual education, and the Teacher Corps
program. In those projects funded over the past decade by the
Administration for Children, Youth and Families (Head Start
Bureau), and by Title VII of the Elementary and Secondary
Education Act, for example, the emphasis in the required
evaluation of effects has been on the acquisition of English by

students of limited English proficiency, and on the relationship
of increased proficiency to the students' performance on
standardized tests of academic achievement (e.g., Chesterfield and
Chavez, 1982; and Martinez, De Gaetano, Williams, and Volk, 1985).
Some work has been done on the evaluation of the implementation of
particular approaches (e.g., Williams, Harrington, and De Gaetano,
1979; Williams, De Gaetano, and Arjona, 1980; and Williams and
Cruikshank, 1981), but those works have remained in the realm of
unpublished project reports.

Characterization of Available Resources

Available multicultural resources can be characterized
according to type (i.e., programs, curricula, teaching strategies
or learning materials resources), with note of the orientation or
approach to multicultural education that they embody, and the
elements of program or curriculum design that they incorporate.
This procedure can help consumers select the particular works that
will best suit their purpose.

Among the multicultural programs now available for use in
early childhood settings, are four resulting from a call to action
funded by the Administration for Children, Youth and Families (The
Head Start Strategy for Spanish-speaking Children, later extended
to concerns of multicultural education) from 1975 through 1980.
The works of Cox, Macauley, and Ramirez (1982), Hanes, Flores,
Rosario, Weikart, and Sanchez (1979), Williams, De Gaetano,
Harrington, and Sutherland (1985), and Zamora (1985), were
developed under this federal sponsorship. While the programs were
first conceived by the funding agency as targeted toward children
who were culturally different, they evolved into orientations that
would now more properly be described as multicultural education.

All four programs employ processes that can be applied across
cultural and linguistic groups, and contain all of the elements of
program/curriculum design. Specific examples of learning
activities are given, along with descriptions of teaching
strategies, suggestions for classroom materials, staff development
exercises, parent involvement suggestions, and considerations for
project administrators.

The books, guides and manuals produced under different
sponsorship by Bennett (1986), Lynch (1986), Nixon (1985),
Martinez, De Gaetano, Williams, and Volk (1990), Ramsey (1987),
and others cited in the annotations that follow, have the same
characteristics as the four programs described above. Several of
these sources extend the multicultural perspective through the
elementary school grades.

There are now a number of resources available offering curriculum suggestions. Among them are the works of Arora and Duncan (1986), Gay (1979), Gold, Grant, and Rivlin (1977), Kendall (1983), King (1980), Tiedt and Tiedt (1986), and others annotated below. While these works vary in the particular elements of curriculum design they incorporate, they all focus primarily on classroom applications. Across these resources, definitions of culture, inclusion of linguistic and other variations, and orientation or approach to multicultural education vary somewhat.

Works emphasizing teaching strategies in concert with curriculum include Banks (1987), Brandt (1986), Garcia (1982), Gollnick and Chinn (1983), and Seelye (1976), among others. These guidelines, manuals, and books also contain other elements of curriculum design, but are largely focused on the content, nature and quality of child/adult and child/child interactions. Once again, the works vary in orientation or approach to multicultural education.

Classroom materials intended for use in multicultural programs are becoming more readily available, as states have begun to mandate incorporation of multicultural content in school curriculum. These materials include audiovisual aids, games, children's books, flannel board sets, and a few other manipulatives such as puzzles. The final section of the annotations that follow identifies resources useful in the selection of classroom materials for programs infusing a multicultural perspective through all areas of the curriculum.

Critical review of works that claim to incorporate a multicultural perspective, and assessment of the suitability of their use within a particular classroom or district, can be facilitated by use of criteria derived from the considerations explored in this chapter. The first set of criteria below were drawn from those of Sleeter and Grant (1987). The second set is derived from the elements of curriculum/program design. The third set summarizes the materials assessment procedures suggested by Williams, De Gaetano, Harrington, and Sutherland (1985).

Criteria for Selection of Teachers' Guides,
Books and Manuals

Orientation or Approach

1.   Are the materials intended to be used particularly with children from minority populations, to enable those children to succeed in school? (education of the culturally different)

2. Do the materials focus entirely on the culture of a specific ethnic group? (single group studies)
3. Is the primary purpose of the material to encourage intergroup communication and cooperation among all the children? (intergroup relations)
4. Do the materials emphasize the positive, adaptive value of multicultural education, and the appropriateness of their use with all children? (multicultural education)
5. Do the materials address changes in structures of society that inhibit full political, economic, and social participation for all peoples? (education that is multicultural and social reconstructionist)
6. Are the materials self-contained, or do they promote infusion of a multicultural perspective throughout the total curriculum/program?

Suitability of Use of Resources
for a Particular Setting

1. What are the purposes or goals for use of the resource from the author's point of view? (What approach or orientation to multicultural education is embodied in those purposes?)
2. For what population was the resource designed? (What view of the child as a learner is assumed?)
3. What sorts of learning activities are proposed, and how will they articulate with the total program or curriculum?
4. What teaching strategies are proposed, and how will they articulate with the total program or curriculum?
5. What learning materials are recommended for use in the classroom?
6. What mechanisms are suggested for evaluating the effectiveness of the overall approach?
7. What preparation for teachers or other staff is needed for competent use of this resource?

Criteria for Assessing the Appropriateness
of Use of Specific Classroom Materials

1. Do the materials contain positive messages about particular cultural, ethnic, or racial groups, as well as avoid negative messages?
2. Are illustrations of the characters in the materials natural in appearance? Are they accurate?
3. In books, is there avoidance of condescension in the

treatment of minority group story characters?
4. Are the lifestyles of minority group members depicted as
    equal to the lifestyles of majority group members?
5. Do particular words used to describe a minority group member
    convey positive images of the individual?
6. Is the philosophy underlying the presentation in the material
    consonant with the goals and purposes of the multicultural
    approach that you are using?
7. Will the material fit well with the learning activities and
    the teaching strategies that you are proposing to use?

Summary

Existing resources on multicultural programs, curricula, and
teaching strategies can be characterized according to orientation
or approach to multicultural education, type of resource (ranging
from broad programs to classroom learning materials), definitions
of culture, incorporation of other aspects of human variation, and
the elements of program/curriculum design they contain. Consumers
using particular resources should be aware of the many
possibilities that these works can represent, and consequently
select those that best suit their intent.

Broadly conceived, the works discussed in this chapter
represent the translation into educational practice of the
philosophies and policies discussed in Chapter I, and the
understandings of child development reviewed in Chapter II of the
source book. Critical elements the resources have in common are
attention to the contexts of human learning, and recognition that
educators can draw upon those contexts to achieve their desired
aims. It is this latter realization that may point the way to
future research and development in the field.

References

Arora, Ranjit K., and Carlton Duncan (Eds.). Multicultural Education: Towards Good Practice. London: Routledge and Kegan, 1986.

Banks, James A. Teaching Strategies for Ethnic Studies, fourth edition. Boston: Allyn & Bacon, Inc. 1987.

Baratz, Stephen S., and Joan C. Baratz. "Early Childhood Intervention: The Social Science Base of Institutional Racism." Harvard Educational Review 40 (Winter 1970): 29-50.

Bennett, Christine I. Comprehensive Multicultural Education: Theory and Practice. Boston: Allyn & Bacon, Inc. 1986.

Bloom, Benjamin S., J. Thomas Hastings, and George F. Madaus. Handbook on Formative and Summative Evaluation of Student Learning. New York: McGraw-Hill Book Company, 1971.

Brandt, Godfrey L. The Realization of Anti-Racist Teaching. London: The Falmer Press, 1986.

Chesterfield, Ray, and Regino Chavez. "An Evaluation of the Head Start Bilingual Bicultural Curriculum Development Project." Final report. Los Angeles: Juarez and Associates, 1982.

Cox, Barbara G., Janet Macauley, and Manuel Ramirez III. Nuevas Fronteras/New Frontiers. New York: Pergamon Press, 1982.

Epstein, Charlotte. Intergroup Relations for the Classroom Teacher. New York: Houghton Mifflin, 1968.

Garcia, Ricardo. Teaching in a Pluralistic Society. New York: Harper & Row Publishers, 1982.

Gay, Geneva. "On Behalf of Children: A Curriculum Design for Multicultural Education in the Elementary School." Journal of Negro Education 48 (1979): 324-40.

Gelfand, Mary. "A Day in the Life: An Exploratory Study of Daily Life of Two Primary Level Classroom Teachers." Doctoral Dissertation. Teachers College, Columbia University, 1988.

Gimmestad, Beverly J., and Edith De Chiara. "Dramatic Plays: A Vehicle for Prejudice Reduction in the Elementary School." Journal of Educational Research 76 (1982): 45-49.

Gold, Milton J., Carl A. Grant, and Harry Rivlin (Eds.). In Praise of Diversity: A Resource Book for Multicultural Education. Washington, D.C.: Teacher Corps and Association of Teacher Educators, 1977.

Gollnick, Donna M., and Philip C. Chinn. Multicultural Education in a Pluralistic Society. St. Louis: C.V. Mosby, 1983.

Grambs, Jean D. Intergroup Education: Methods and Materials. Englewood Cliffs, NJ: Prentice-Hall, 1968.

Grant, Carl A., and Christine E. Sleeter. "The Literature on Multicultural Education: Review and Analysis." Photocopy. Madison, WI: University of Wisconsin, 1984.

Gray, Susan W., Rupert A. Klaus, James O. Miller, and Bettye J. Forrester. Before First Grade. New York: Teachers College Press, 1966.

Hanes, Michael L., Marina I. Flores, Jose Rosario, David P. Weikart, and Jose Sanchez. Un Marco Abierto: An Open Framework for Educators. Ypsilanti, MI: High/Scope Educational Research Foundation, 1979.

Kendall, Frances E. Diversity in the Classroom: A Multicultural Approach to the Education of Young Children. New York: Teachers College Press, 1983.

King, Edith W. Teaching Ethnic Awareness: Methods and Materials for the Elementary School. Santa Monica, CA: Goodyear Publishing Company, Inc., 1980.

Lynch, James. Teaching in the Multicultural School. London: Ward Lock Educational, 1981.

Martinez, Herminio, Yvonne De Gaetano, Leslie R. Williams, and
     Dinah Volk. "Evaluation Report of the Cross-Cultural
     Demonstration Project." Final Report. New York: Institute
     for Urban and Minority Education, Teachers College, 1985.

Martinez, Herminio, Yvonne De Gaetano, Leslie R. Williams, and
     Dinah Volk. Kaleidoscope: A Cross-Cultural Approach to
     Teaching and Learning. Menlo Park, CA: Addison-Wesley,
     1990.

Nixon, Jon. A Teacher's Guide to Multicultural Education. New
     York: Basil Blackwell, 1985.

Ramsey, Patricia G. Teaching and Learning in a Diverse World:
     Multicultural Education for Young Children. New York:
     Teachers College Press, 1987.

Sarason, Seymour B. The Culture of the School and the Problem of
     Change. Boston: Allyn & Bacon, Inc., 1982.

Seelye, H. Ned. Teaching Culture: Strategies for Intercultural
     Communication. Lincolnwood, IL: National Textbook Company,
     1986.

Slavin, Robert E. "Integrating the Desegregated Classroom."
     Educational Leadership (February, 1979): 322-24.

Sleeter, Christine E., and Carl A. Grant. "An Analysis of
     Multicultural Education in the United States." Harvard
     Educational Review 57 (1987): 421-44.

Taba, Hilda, Elizabeth Hall Brady, and John T. Robinson.
     Intergroup Education in Public Education. Washington, DC:
     American Council on Education, 1982.

Tiedt, Pamela L., and Iris M. Tiedt. Multicultural Teaching: A
     Handbook of Activities, Information and Resources, second
     edition. Boston: Allyn & Bacon, Inc., 1986.

Valentine, Charles A. "Deficit, Difference, and Bicultural Models
     of Afro-American Behavior." Harvard Educational Review 41
     (May, 1971): 137-57.

Williams, John. "Perspectives on the Multicultural Curriculum."
     Social Science Teacher 8 (April 1979): 249-56.

Williams, Leslie R., and Susan B. Cruikshank. "Assessing the
     Adequacy of the Implementation of a Program Innovation: An
     Exploration of Methods Used in Selected Preschool Settings in
     Relation to Research on Change in the Elementary School."

Commissioned Report. Washington, D.C.: National Institute of
Education, 1981.

Williams, Leslie R., Yvonne De Gaetano, and Leila Arjona.
"Training and Technical Assistance in the Implementation of
ALERTA: An Analysis of Process." Final Report. New York:
Institute for Urban and Minority Education, Teachers College,
1980.

Williams, Leslie R., Yvonne De Gaetano, Charles C. Harrington, and
Iris R. Sutherland. ALERTA: A Multicultural, Bilingual
Approach to Teaching Young Children. Menlo Park, CA:
Addison-Wesley, 1985.

Williams, Leslie R., Charles C. Harrington, and Yvonne De Gaetano.
"Third Annual Report of the ALERTA Curriculum Research and
Development Project." Final Report. New York: Institute for
Urban and Minority Education, Teachers College, 1979.

Yinger, Robert. "A Study of Teacher Planning." The Elementary
School Journal 80 (1) (1980): 107-27.

Yonemura, Margaret. A Teacher at Work. New York: Teachers
College Press, 1986.

Zamora, Gloria Rodriguez. Nuevo Amanecer/New Dawn. Lincolnwood,
IL: National Textbook Company, 1985.

Bibliography

Entries in this bibliography are arranged alphabetically under four major headings: Programs, Curricula, Teaching Strategies, and Learning Materials Resources. The four categories are not mutually exclusive, but the works do tend to emphasize one type of resource over others. The individual annotations will therefore first appear in the category that each predominantly represents, and then will be cross-referenced to other categories as appropriate.

Programs

74. Bennett, Christine I. Comprehensive Multicultural Education: Theory and Practice. Boston: Allyn & Bacon, Inc. 1986.

Examines the conversion of theory into practice through consideration of the definitions, assumptions, and goals that underlie multicultural education. Beginning with presentation of the kinds of knowledge needed by teachers to implement a multicultural perspective, Bennett moves to suggestion of teaching strategies that make use of such knowledge, and provides specific examples of infusion of cultural content across curriculum areas. While the book is designed largely for use by secondary school teachers, there are sufficient examples of applications in upper elementary grades to make the work a valuable addition to the resources for teachers of middleschool children. Bennett's discussion of the dynamic between individual and group (cultural) differences, and her review of teachers' possible misperceptions of children's behavior are especially thought-provoking.

75. Chud, Gyda, and Ruth Fahlman, with Reena Baker and Patricia Wakefield. Early Childhood Education for a Multicultural Society: A Handbook for Educators.

Vancouver: Western Education Development Group, Faculty
of Education, The University of British Columbia, 1985.

A one-volume program resource for administrators and
teachers working at the preschool level. The authors lay
the foundations for program development in the attitudes,
knowledge, and skills of the adults delivering educational
services to culturally diverse children. Moving from
teacher introspection to strategies for working with parents
and making home-school connections, they illustrate concrete
ways to foster second language acquisition and continued
development in the physical, emotional, social, and
intellectual domains. Preparation of the classroom
environment and the content of learning activities are
derived from analysis of the cultural traditions brought by
individual children to the classroom, and from attention to
the children's present, everyday experience. Concepts and
skills arising from these sources are arranged into thematic
presentations. Teaching strategies aimed at confronting
prejudices and stereotyping are also included.

76. Cox, Barbara G., Janet Macauley, and Manuel Ramirez III.
      Nuevas Fronteras/New Frontiers. New York: Pergamon
      Press, 1982.

A multicultural program for the early childhood years,
arranged in a set that includes two handbooks for teachers
(one on young children's learning in a multicultural
context, and one on the specifics of program
implementation), instructional unit plans, and classroom
learning materials, such as storybooks and accompanying
flannelboard pieces. The work integrates traditional
attention to the socioemotional, psychomotor, and cognitive/
linguistic development of young children, with awareness of
possible variation in learning and teaching behaviors that
may affect concept and skill acquisition. Originally field
tested in the Southwest region of the United States, the
program draws a number of its examples from Mexican-American
culture, but integrates cultural content from other groups
as well. Highly specified teacher procedures are provided
as a vehicle for teacher preparation for use of the program.

77. Foerster, Leona. "Moving from Ethnic Studies to
      Multi-cultural Education." The Urban Review 14 (1982):
      121-26.

Offers guidelines for creating educational programs
that infuse a multicultural perspective throughout the K-12
curriculum. Foerster emphasizes the need to address
teachers' feelings about the proposed multicultural
orientation, as well as to provide the specific knowledge,
skill development, and resources needed for design of
multicultural learning activities. Teacher ownership in the
process of program development, reflection of the cultural
configurations of the local community (as well as the
possibly greater diversity of American society), and a well
developed inservice teacher education plan, are seen as
potent prerequisites for program implementation, and as ways
of avoiding the limitations that brought about a decrease in
use of ethnic studies over the past decade.

78. Gay, Geneva. "What is Your School's MEQ?" Educational
     Leadership 39 (1981): 187-89.

Guidelines for assessing the degree to which a
multicultural perspective permeates the total school
environment. Gay presents a list of 45 criteria for
determining a school's "multicultural education quotient"
grouped under the following areas of operation: curriculum
and instruction, staffing, support services, student
activities, and school climate. As with programs
themselves, Gay notes, adequate assessment of use of a
multicultural perspective must be holistic and systemic.

79. Hanes, Michael L., Marina I. Flores, Jose Rosario, David P.
     Weikart, and Jose Sanchez. Un Marco Abierto: An Open
     Framework for Educators. Ypsilanti, MI.: High/Scope
     Educational Research Foundation, 1979.

A set of early childhood program materials, including a
guide for teachers, a guide for parents, handout booklets
for parents, and filmstrips on aspects of use of the program
for teachers and for parents. The program is a
multicultural adaptation of the Piagetian-based early
childhood approach developed by Weikart and his associates
in the early 1970s. Ways to promote continuing development
of young children's concepts of classification, seriation,
number, and spatial and temporal relations through use of
"key experiences" in preparation of the classroom
environment, and in child/child and child/adult
interactions, are emphasized. The guides contain

descriptions of processes for working with parents, and for preparing staff for program implementation.

80. Lynch, James. The Multicultural Curriculum. London: Batsford Academic and Educational, Ltd., 1983.

Presents an overall program design for introduction of a multicultural perspective into the public school across grade levels. While Lynch is describing the circumstances of the British school system in particular, many of the processes he describes would be equally applicable in the United States. In addition to providing a well articulated rationale for use of a multicultural perspective in education, he outlines a framework for constructing a multicultural curriculum that would be most helpful to program planners, and offers guidelines for actions to assist planners through the maze of decision-making that is part of the overall process. Guidance for individual teachers in the form of suggested approaches, teaching strategies and planning procedures is also included.

81. Martinez, Herminio, Yvonne De Gaetano, Leslie R. Williams, and Dinah Volk. Kaleidoscope: A Cross-Cultural Approach to Teaching and Learning. Menlo Park, CA: Addison-Wesley, 1990.

A multicultural program designed for use in kindergarten through grade six in the public school. The program materials consist of two source books for teachers (Source Book 1: Kindergarten - Grade Three, and Source Book 2: Grade Four - Grade Six) and an accompanying staff development guide. Kaleidoscope illustrates a process for integrating cultural content across subject areas at each grade level, so that the knowledge children bring with them to the classroom may be used as points of departure in teaching new concepts and critical thinking skills. Each source book contains material on children's developmental stages, cultural contexts, and second language acquisition, and abundant examples of integration of cultural content in traditional subject areas (language arts, mathematics, science, social studies, and second language learning). A variety of connections are drawn among the subject areas in suggested extensions of the learning activities. The staff development guide provides complete descriptions of workshops to involve parents in the instructional process, and to prepare staff for implementation of the approach.

82. Nixon, Jon. A Teacher's Guide to Multicultural Education.
    New York: Basil Blackwell, 1985.

    Examines an overall program for infusing multicultural
    education throughout a school system. Nixon gives an
    excellent analysis of the forces that have fueled racism in
    Great Britain, and offers both rationale and strategies for
    addressing the need for change within the system. The work
    provides many important insights for program developers
    around the issues of relationships among the key players
    within the schools, parent and community involvement, and
    evaluation and ongoing elaboration of the program. For
    individual teachers, the chapters on classroom approaches
    and language issues may be most helpful. The suggestions
    provided can be applied at the upper elementary school
    level, as well as in higher grades. While Nixon recognizes
    the importance of use of classroom materials reflecting a
    multicultural perspective, he emphasizes that how a subject
    is taught, the degree to which a multicultural point of view
    is manifested, is likely to be more important than the
    materials themselves.

83. Ramsey, Patricia G. Teaching and Learning in a Diverse
    World: Multicultural Education for Young Children. New
    York: Teachers College Press, 1987.

    Emphasizes the appropriateness of integration of a
    multicultural perspective throughout the curriculum for all
    children, particularly for those whose exposure to people
    from diverse populations may be limited, and therefore may
    be in danger of developing stereotypic characterizations.
    Focusing on the possibilities in programs of early childhood
    education, Ramsey analyzes the perceptions shaped by both
    developmental levels and lack of extended experience which
    young children are likely to bring to the learning setting,
    and makes specific suggestions for curriculum construction
    in the preparation of the classroom environment, expansion
    of physical knowledge through exposure to diversity in
    materials, and celebration of holidays with variation in
    mind. Work with parents, and the preparation of teachers
    essential in carrying out the proposed program, are also
    discussed.

84. Widlake, Paul. Reducing Educational Disadvantage. Milton
    Keynes, U.K.: Open University Press, 1986.

Describes and discusses the processes involved in the development of multicultural educational programs in Britain in the 1970s and 1980s. Widlake traces the move from a compensatory model to what he terms a "communications" model that stresses parent participation. Parents from culturally diverse communities were systematically involved in determination of instructional goals and in working collaboratively with teachers in the delivery of instructional services. Results of the interventions were positive, as assessed by children's performance on standardized measures of reading and other academic skills, and by observation of changes over time in attitudes expressed by teachers and community members. The descriptions focus largely on work done in preschool and elementary school settings.

85. Williams, Leslie R., Yvonne De Gaetano, Charles C. Harrington, and Iris R. Sutherland. ALERTA: A Multicultural, Bilingual Approach to Teaching Young Children. Menlo Park, CA: Addison-Wesley, 1985.

A guide for early childhood teachers, administrators, staff developers, and parent involvement workers wishing to infuse a multicultural perspective throughout an educational program for three- to five-year-olds. Designed for use in diverse settings (public school, Head Start centers, private school, day care, etc.), ALERTA is organized into nine levels of program implementation, moving from information-sharing among the adults in the program, to processes for determining cultural and community content of activities, to planning and organization of the curriculum, to specific teaching strategies, and finally, to techniques of assessment and evaluation. For each level of implementation, background information is provided, and staff/parent development exercises are described. Examples of applications in activities for children are given to illustrate the various levels of implementation, and resources for ongoing program development are suggested. The processes presented can be utilized with any cultural and/or linguistic group.

86. Youngblood, Chester E. "Multicultural Early Childhood Education." Viewpoints in Teaching and Learning 55 (1979): 37-43.

Argues for multicultural education for all children as a way of broadening children's experience in a guided

manner, encouraging positive assumption of ethnic
affiliations, and valuing the recognition and sharing of
diversity within our society. The author identifies four
major obstacles to multicultural program implementation
(separation of young children by race and socioeconomic
status, lack of appropriate teacher preparation, scarcity of
multicultural curriculum materials suitable for use with
young children, and subsuming multicultural approaches into
bilingual programs designed for non-white children), and
discusses why each of these is an inadequate response to
cultural diversity. The article concludes with presentation
of eight procedures to apply in infusing a multicultural
perspective throughout educational programs for young
children.

87. Zamora, Gloria Rodriguez. Nuevo Amanecer/New Dawn.
     Lincolnwood, IL: National Textbook Company, 1985.

     A set of three manuals for teachers containing a
detailed management system to enable early childhood staff
to put a multicultural program into place in their classroom
or center. Ways are presented to assess the children's
incoming knowledge and skills, record their ongoing
acquisition of skills and concepts, and select or plan
learning activities on the basis of that information.
Communication with parents and their participation in the
carrying out of the classroom activities, as well as other
forms of community involvement, are encouraged through the
use of informative notes sent home with the children and
conversations during home visits. The manuals offer plans
for arrangement of classrooms, selection of materials,
teaching strategies, and sample learning activities.

Curricula

88. Arora, Ranjit K., and Carlton G. Duncan (Eds.).
     Multicultural Education: Towards Good Practice.
     London: Routledge and Kegan Paul, 1986.

     An exploration of the British multicultural educational
experience, with a variety of chapters devoted to examples
of curriculum applications. The chapters written by Arora
(on curriculum processes for the primary grades), Collicot
(multicultural approaches to mathematics), Watts (science
education from a multicultural perspective), and Klein (on
choice of multicultural resources) all offer suggestions
useful to teachers of primary and upper elementary school

children. The emphasis throughout the work is on addressing
societal structures that promote continuing discrimination
and inequality of opportunity in culturally diverse
populations.

89. Baker, Gwendolyn C., Marshall Brody, Clarence Beecher, and
     Robert P. Ho. "Modifying Curriculums to Meet
     Multicultural Needs." Teaching in a Multicultural
     Society. Edited by Delores E. Cross, Gwendolyn C.
     Baker, and Lindley J. Stiles. New York: The Free
     Press, 1977.

     Traces the ways classroom curricula can be reformulated
to reflect a multicultural perspective suitable for use with
all children. The authors recommend first, the
establishment of a knowledge base through use of such
resources as children's books and increasingly available
audio-visual materials (carefully reviewed ahead of time for
accuracy in presentation and avoidance of stereotyping).
Their second step is selection of teaching strategies, and
their third, the choice of a curriculum design that
reflects, at a deep level, the goals the teacher wishes to
achieve. The authors contend that existing curricula can be
modified into successful multicultural presentations, but
that close attention must be given to the articulation of
each of the curricular elements, so that the children
experience a coherent whole. Examples of applications
spanning the elementary school years are provided to
illustrate the points made.

90. Bennett, Christine I. Comprehensive Multicultural
     Education: Theory and Practice   (item 74).

91. Booth, Tony and David Coulby (Eds.). Producing and Reducing
     Disaffection: Curricula for All. Milton Keynes,
     England: Open University Press, 1987.

     A collection of essays exploring ways to reach children
and young people who have been judged to be "unteachable" in
traditional British classrooms. Several essays in the work
allude to or discuss antiracist pedagogy as an alternative
to present approaches, and, additionally, examine the
content of curricula to illustrate the perpetuation of
stereotypes. Of particular interest in this regard are the
contributions of Wright (on racism in learning materials)
and Singh (on racism in the curriculum as a whole). The

orientation of the total work is toward the social
reconstructionist point of view.

92. Chud, Gyda, and Ruth Fahlman, with Reena Baker and Patricia
    Wakefield. Early Childhood Education for a
    Multicultural Society: A Handbook for Educators   (item
    75).

93. Cox, Barbara G., Janet Macauley, and Manuel Ramirez III.
    Nuevas Fronteras/New Frontiers   (item 76).

94. Forman, Sheila, and Ron Mitchell. "The Hawaii Multicultural
    Awareness Pilot Project (HMAP)." Educational
    Perspectives 16 (4) (December, 1977): 26-28.

    Presents the initial results of the HMAP curriculum
development project. The work of the project was focused on
the instructional program and the design of particular
materials, teaching strategies, and learning activities
aimed at enhancing intercultural understanding and
appreciation. At the upper elementary level, the project
concentrated on the design of units intended to provide a
multicultural perspective in the social studies offered
fourth, fifth and sixth-graders. Instead of a then more
commonly used ethnic studies approach, the project used
themes seen to represent "cultural universals," such as
lifecycle and community celebrations (fourth grade), family
(fifth grade), and school communities (sixth grade). The
thematic approach was extended to foster the interweaving of
topics, cross-cultural student interaction of students, and
individualization and personalization of learning, as well
as other teaching strategies.

95. Gay, Geneva. "On Behalf of Children: A Curriculum Design
    for Multicultural Education in the Elementary School."
    Journal of Negro Education 48 (1979):324-40.

    Explores mechanisms for integrating a multicultural
perspective throughout the elementary school, so that it
becomes totally integrated into all subject and skill areas
addressed. Beginning with a powerful rationale for change
of orientation in the elementary school toward active
recognition of cultural diversity, Gay proceeds to examine
the implications for practice of that point of view. She
looks at each of the elements of curriculum design

(diagnostic techniques, skills to be mastered, content and
materials, learning activities, teaching behaviors, and
evaluation procedures) in relation to each other and in
relation to the ways each should reflect a multicultural
approach. Specific procedures for carrying out the process
of integration are described.

96. Hanes, Michael L., Marina I. Flores, Jose Rosario, David P.
     Weikart and Jose Sanchez. Un Marco Abierto: An Open
     Framework for Educators (item 79).

97. Kendall, Frances E. Diversity in the Classroom: A
     Multicultural Approach to the Education of Young
     Children. New York: Teachers College Press, 1983.

     Uses the developmental-interaction approach to
     curriculum formulation articulated by Biber and Shapiro at
     the Bank Street College of Education, in combination with
     Taba's emphasis on promotion of human relations, to propose
     curriculum guidelines for use in classrooms serving young
     children. Kendall's goal is to reduce racism through
     affirmation of cultural diversity with all children in the
     activities provided, the selection of learning materials,
     and the traditional early childhood curriculum emphases
     (blockbuilding, language experiences, art activities, etc.).
     Examples of unit planning are provided along with a variety
     of resource lists.

98. King, Edith W. Teaching Ethnic Awareness: Methods and
     Materials for the Elementary School. Santa Monica, CA:
     Goodyear Publishing Company, Inc. 1980.

     Supports the positive recognition of pluralism in
     American society by introduction of multiethnic studies from
     the early primary through the upper elementary school years.
     The first half of the book offers a rationale for the study,
     provides background information on ethnic diversity, and
     describes basic teaching strategies that have been
     demonstrated to be effective in multiethnic presentations.
     The second half of the work contains many examples of
     activities (ascending in order from kindergarten to those
     appropriate for the upper elementary grades) that reflect
     and draw upon children's increasing sophistication regarding
     individual and group variation. King notes that the design
     of learning activities must attend carefully to children's
     developmental levels, both in regard to their cognitive

processes and socioemotional responses.   That awareness is
illustrated through the specification of objectives for the
sample activities, and through the choice of teaching
materials in each instance.

99. Martinez, Herminio, Yvonne De Gaetano, Leslie R. Williams,
     and Dinah Volk. Kaleidoscope: A Cross-Cultural
     Approach to Teaching and Learning   (item 81).

100. Ramsey, Patricia G. "Multicultural Education in Early
      Childhood." Young Children 37 (2) (January, 1982):
      13-24.

      Discusses four common misconceptions about
multicultural education, namely, that multicultural
education should focus on information about other countries
and cultures, that multicultral education is only relevant
in classrooms that are obviously culturally and/or racially
diverse, that there should be a single set of goals and
curriculum for multicultural education, and that
multicultural education can be simply added on to an
existing curriculum. Ramsey challenges each misconception,
and provides alternative learning activities to introduce
the concept of diversity to young children. The importance
of creating connections and continuity with children's
previous experience, and of teacher preparation in the form
of examination of one's own attitudes and assumptions, is
emphasized.

101. Ramsey, Patricia G. Teaching and Learning in a Diverse
      World: Multicultural Education for Young Children
      (item 83).

102. Sizemore, Barbara A. "The Four M Curriculum: A Way to Shape
      the Future." Journal of Negro Education 48 (1979):
      341-56.

      Identifies an appropriate approach to the problem of
inequality in education as one of allowing and encouraging
children to reach educational goals through different paths
that recognize the uniqueness of each individual. A
corollary of that position is that, in today's culturally
diverse society, Anglocentric perspectives on the curriculum
must be abandoned in favor of a "Four M" approach to
curriculum making, focusing on education that is
multilingual, multicultural, multimodal and

multidimensional. In this instance, curriculum is defined as the total educational environment, including "what is taught (content), how it is taught (methodology), and how it is organized for implementation (administration)." Implications of the total approach for the structures of schools and for the assessment of student performance are examined.

103. Suzuki, Bob H. "Curriculum Transformation for Multicultural Education." Education and Urban Society 16 (1984): 294-322.

Advocates a social reconstructionist approach to the reformulation of curriculum. Arguing that the permeation of multicultural ideas throughout the educational experience cannot do other than address societal change, the author suggests goals for students and teachers, and ten guiding principles for transforming theory into educational practice, namely (1) starting where people are by incorporating children's experiences into the planning of learning activities, (2) helping people decenter (from their own ethnocentric perspectives), (3) approaching curriculum transformation as a long-term process, (4) viewing multicultural education as integrative, comprehensive, and conceptual in scope, (5) producing changes in the teaching practices and social structures of a classroom, as well as in curriculum content, (6) raising issues that are personally relevant to students, (7) helping students increase their academic achievement through sensitive and relevant teaching approaches and materials, (8) involving parents and utilizing multicultural community resources, (9) dealing with the social and historical realities of American society, and (10) exhibiting care, understanding, concern, and sensitivity toward students. Suzuki concludes with a discussion of the policy implications of those principles for teacher education programs and for educational research, as well as for curriculum making.

104. Tiedt, Pamela L. and Iris M. Tiedt. Multicultural Teaching: A Handbook of Activities, Information and Resources, second edition. Boston: Allyn & Bacon, Inc. 1986.

Designed for use by primary and upper elementary school teachers. Tiedt and Tiedt's orientation is toward child-centered teaching, preferably in open settings, although their suggestions could be applied in more traditional settings as well. Acting on their understanding

that positive self-esteem (and esteem for others) undergirds
effective teaching and genuine learning, the authors begin
with suggestions for activities that strengthen children's
motivation to engage themselves in the learning process.
They then move on to examine the nature of diversity in
society, and to use those notions of diversity in the study
of traditional school subjects, such as language arts and
social studies. The book alternates between providing
specific information on a wide variety of
cultural/linguistic groups, and illustrating use of that
informaton in sample classroom activities. The procedures a
teacher might use to present the activities are woven into
the activity descriptions, and extensive resource and
classroom materials lists appear at the end of the work.

105. Williams, Leslie R., Yvonne De Gaetano, Charles C.
        Harrington, and Iris R. Sutherland. ALERTA: A
        Multicultural, Bilingual Approach to Teaching Young
        Children (item 85).

106. Zamora, Gloria Rodriguez. Nuevo Amanecer/New Dawn (item
        87).

Teaching Strategies

107. Banks, James A. Teaching Strategies for Ethnic Studies,
        fourth edition. Boston: Allyn & Bacon, Inc., 1987.

        The fourth edition of a work representing a shift away
from single group studies to permeation of ethnic studies
throughout the curriculum, as an aspect of total curriculum
reform. Banks provides specific historical and sociological
information on a wide variety of Native American (including
Native Hawaiian), Afro-American, European American, Hispanic
American, and Asian American ethnic groups. Use of the
information in teaching strategies aimed at the primary and
intermediate grades (as well as the upper grades and high
school) across subject areas is illustrated through
description of appropriate learning activities. The book is
rich in resources pertaining to each of the groups
considered.

108. Bennett, Christine I. Comprehensive Multicultural
        Education: Theory and Practice (item 74).

109. Booth, Tony, and David Coulby (Editors). Producing an
        Reducing Disaffection: Curricula for All (item 91).

110. Brandt, Godfrey L. The Realization of Anti-Racist Teaching.
        London: The Falmer Press, 1986.

        A social reconstructionist text drawing upon a "Black
   Third World definition of social reality in racist British
   society and a Black tradition and critique of white European
   scholarship..." The author contends that the present day
   writings of much of the multicultural education movement do
   not fundamentally address the deep social structures that
   continue to disenfranchise people of color in Western
   societies. After discussing the sociohistorical background
   to current debates in Britain and analyzing the contexts for
   reorientation to anti-racist education, Brandt illustrates
   how common lessons can be prepared to reflect an anti-racist
   point of view. In this, he feels he moves beyond the simpler
   demands of multicultural education itself. Similarly,
   Brandt examines the reformulation of teaching strategies to
   eliminate bias in subtler forms of classroom communication.

111. Chud, Gyda and Ruth Fahlman, with Reena Baker and Patricia
        Wakefield. Early Childhood Education for a
        Multicultural Society: A Handbook for Educators (item
        75).

112. Cox, Barbara G., Janet Macauley, and Manuel Ramirez III.
        Nuevas Fronteras/New Frontiers (item 76).

113. DeCosta, Sandra B. "Not All Children are Anglo and Middle
        Class: A Practical Beginning for the Elementary
        Teacher." Theory into Practice 23 (1984): 155-62.

        Argues that teachers are usually inadequately prepared
   to meet the diversity typical of today's classrooms, and
   that they therefore must proceed independently toward the
   knowledge, attitudes, skills, and characteristics needed for
   multicultural teaching. This article is intended to provide
   a beginning for elementary school teachers by suggesting
   strategies and generic learning activities that can be
   adapted according to regional and cultural differences, and
   the life patterns of the children in particular classrooms.
   (Adaptation would also need to be made according to the
   developmental and grade levels of the children.) The

teacher's fostering of his or her own level of awareness, comprehension of the specifics of diversity, and eventual inclusion of multicultural perspectives across subject areas in the curriculum are seen as critical to the success of the proposed teaching strategies.

114. Garcia, Ricardo L. "Countering Classroom Discrimination." Theory into Practice 23 (1984): 104-9.

Provides strategies for countering stereotypes of gender, race, ethnicity, or social class that arise in societies due to ignorance, unpleasant incidents, folk wisdom socialization, hard times, or internal colonialization. Garcia's premise is that teachers can make a difference for themselves and the children they serve by, first, honestly examining their own attitudes and beliefs, and subsequently, recognizing the extent of their own ethnocentrism. Stereotypes caused by ignorance, hard times, and folk wisdom socialization may be countered by providing accurate information. Stereotypes arising from unpleasant incidents or colonialism may be best addressed through simulations or other forms of role play. Most importantly, teachers can counter discrimination by expecting excellence from all their students, and can support that expectation by maintaining high standards of performance.

115. Garcia, Ricardo L. Teaching in a Pluralistic Society. New York: Harper & Row Publishers, 1982.

Presents two instructional models (ethnic studies and bilingual education) and two instructonal strategies (human rights and intergroup relations) designed to permeate classrooms with awareness of the positive implications of cultural diversity. While Garcia sees each of these elements as having a discrete function, he advocates using all or several of them together in a synthesis for deepest effect. The first half of the work is devoted to discussion of the concepts and issues (such as definition of ethnicity and culture, societal stages in movement toward recognition of cultural diversity, and the intersection of the structures of schools and communities with the purposes behind teaching from a pluralistic perspective) that have given the movement impetus. The book's second half offers many specific suggestions for both models and both strategies that are suitable for use with middle and upper elementary school children. They can also be adapted for

secondary school projects. Permeation of the pluralistic
perspective across all subject areas is stressed.

116. Gimmestad, Beverly J., and Edith De Chiara. "Dramatic
        Plays: A Vehicle for Prejudice Reduction in the
        Elementary School." Journal of Educational Research 76
        (1982): 45-49.

        Describes a study designed to reduce prejudice among
fourth, fifth, and sixth graders by incorporation of
dramatic plays about four ethnic groups (Black, Hispanic,
Jewish, and Chinese) into the classroom curriculum. The
experimental children worked in racially/ethnically mixed
groups on tasks assigned in relation to reading and enacting
four plays (one on each of the four ethnic groups). Pre-
and post-tests of knowledge about attitudes toward the four
groups yielded statistically significant results when the
performances of the experimental children were compared with
those of the controls. The authors conclude that when
small, ethnically heterogeneous groups of children work
together on a task where some measure of success is
forthcoming, the group members are likely to develop
positive attitudes toward each other.

117. Gollnick, Donna M. and Philip C. Chinn. Multicultural
        Education in a Pluralistic Society. St. Louis: C.V.
        Mosby, 1983.

        A resource book devoted largely to the provision of
detailed background information on the specifics of cultural
pluralism (religion, language, ethnicity, gender, etc.)
needed in order for teachers successfully to implement
multicultural teaching strategies. Gollnick and Chinn
explore the complexity of each dimension of diversity, with
attention to intragroup as well as cross-group variation.
The cumulative effect is to sensitize the reader to the
issues and to clarify questions one should ask when
preparing to teach in culturally diverse circumstances. The
final chapter of the work discusses instructional
strategies, suggesting general guidelines helpful to
teachers who are beginning to initiate the approach in their
classrooms.

118. Hanes, Michael L., Marina I. Flores, Jose Rosario, David P.
        Weikart, and Jose Sanchez. Un Marco Abierto: An Open
        Framework for Educators (item 79).

119. King, Edith W. Teaching Ethnic Awareness: Methods and
         Materials for the Elementary School   (item 98).

120. Kitano, Margie K. "Early Education for Asian American
         Children." Young Children 35 (2) (January, 1980):
         13-26.

         Reviews cultural factors and learning characteristics
      associated with children of Japanese, Chinese, Filipino,
      Vietnamese, Korean, Hawaiian and Samoan descent, and reports
      on a study designed to determine Asian American children's
      learning styles and competencies prior to their entrance in
      public school. Drawing implications from the work for
      education, the authors reject the "cultural deficit"
      hypothesis in favor of the "cultural difference" model, and
      reiterate the importance of changing teaching practices to
      meet the child's needs. They also point out that teachers
      from the North American mainstream tend to view Asian
      Americans as a monolithic group, whereas substantial
      cultural differences do exist among the various Asian
      groups. Likewise, the differences that exist for
      individuals within a group must also be acknowledged, so
      that stereotyping can be avoided.

121. Lynch, James. The Multicultural Curriculum (item 80).

122. Martinez, Herminio, Yvonne De Gaetano, Leslie R. Williams
         and Dinah Volk. Kaleidoscope: A Cross-Cultural
         Approach to Teaching and Learning (item 81).

123. Ramsey, Patricia G. Teaching and Learning in a Diverse
         World: Multicultural Education for Young Children
         (item 83).

124. Sancho, Anthony R. "Culture in the Bilingual-Bicultural
         Curriculum." NABE 1 (May, 1977): 55-58.

         An early article presaging most of the teaching
      strategies now consistently recommended to foster a
      permeation or infusion approach to multicultural education
      in the classroom. Although originally written to inform
      teachers in bilingual classrooms, Sancho's ten principles
      for creating environments conducive to learning are equally
      applicable in monolingual circumstances. Those principles
      are: defining the classroom as a safe place for children,

presenting the classroom as a multicultural center,
recognizing and acting upon diversity in teaching and
learning style, humanizing instruction and learning,
assuming a counseling rather than a continually direct
instructional role, motivating students by use of their own
interests and previous experiences, using field experiences
to extend learning, utilizing heterogeneous grouping
patterns, and using both peer and cross-age teaching and
learning.

125.   Saracho, Olivia N., and Bernard Spodek (Eds.). Understanding
       the Multicultural Experience in Early Childhood
       Education. Washington, DC: NAEYC, 1983.

       An edited volume that is organized into a three-part
progression: provision of specific information on young
children from four broadly defined cultural groups (Mexican-
American, Black American, American-Indian, and
Asian-American), discussion of multicultural, early
childhood educational practices and materials, and review of
the knowledge and skills needed for implementation of a
multicultural approach in early childhood classrooms. The
reader should exercise some caution in not overgeneralizing
from the information provided in the first part of the book,
as the scope of each chapter has generally not allowed full
discussion of intragroup variability. Within the
American-Indian "group," for example, there is enormous
variation in custom according to the Native American nation
of origin. The second section of the book, on educational
practices and materials, raises some important
considerations for teachers of young children regarding ways
to avoid an "add-on" approach through preparation of the
total learning environment, careful selection of learning
materials, and on-going parent and community involvement in
operation of the early childhood program.

126.   Seelye, Ned H. Teaching Culture: Strategies for Foreign
       Language Educators. Skokie, IL: National Textbook
       Company, 1976.

       Written for teachers of foreign languages, this book
illustrates in fascinating ways how language is permeated by
culture, and how language teaching outside of the contexts
in which the language was developed over time, is likely to
result in students unable to achieve genuine fluency. The
work is broadly aimed at secondary school teaching, but
teachers in the upper elementary grades may find this to be
a most valuable resource in designing learning activities

that make students aware of the powerful role of culture in
their lives. The integration of cultural content across
subject areas, and the role of language in teaching and
learning are emphasized.

127. Stahl, Abraham. "Introducing Ethnic Materials to the
        Classroom: Problems and Challenge." Urban Education
        20 (1985): 257-71.

        Reviews the difficulties encountered when Israeli
educators began to use ethnically oriented teaching
materials and curriculum content in classes containing
children of Oriental Jewish heritage. Patterns very similar
to those exhibited in the United States appeared during the
period when the teachers were first trying out the strategy.
It soon became evident that the success of the initiative
depended on the willingness of the individual teachers to
extend their background knowledge, and on the attitudes
conveyed by those teachers as the materials were used. The
tendencies to, first, add on an ethnic studies component to
an existing curriculum, and second, to fail to make
connections between the teaching materials and aspects of
the children's lives, were seen as dangers in the process of
program implementation. In spite of the problems
encountered, the authors see progress in the move toward a
more multicultural approach in Israeli curricula.

128. Suzuki, Bob H. "Curriculum Transformation for Multicultural
        Education." Education and Urban Society (item 103).

129. Widlake, Paul. Reducing Educational Disadvantage (item
        84).

130. Williams, Leslie R. "Teaching from a Multicultural
        Perspective: Some Thoughts on Uses of Diversity."
        Teacher Renewal: Professional Issues, Personal
        Choices. Edited by Frances S. Bolin and Judith
        McConnell Falk. New York: Teachers College Press,
        1987.

        Introduces use of a multicultural perspective to
teachers who may not have been familiar with it previously.
Williams examines the benefits that are likely to result
from incorporation of the perspective, ways to develop the
approach within existing curricula in the schools, and
possibilities for evaluation of both implementation of the

process and its impact upon children in classrooms.
Examples are given of infusion of a multicultural
perspective throughout learning activities at the early
childhood and elementary school levels, as well as
suggestions of principles to follow in selecting materials
for classroom use.

131. Williams, Leslie R., Yvonne De Gaetano, Charles C.
        Harrington, and Iris R. Sutherland. ALERTA: A
        Multicultural, Bilingual Approach to Teaching Young
        Children (item 85).

132. Wolfgang, Aaron. "The Silent Language in the Multicultural
        Classroom." Theory into Practice 26 (1977): 145-52.

        Alerts teachers to possible difficulties in
communication with their students, that may be caused by
three types of non-verbal behavior -- proxemics,
kinesthetics, and paralinguistics (i.e., use of space and
distance in relation to objects and other people, use of
gesture and facial expression, and use of sound features,
such as tone of voice and pauses). All three types of
behavior are understood as culturally acquired repertoires
used to enhance or intensify verbal exchanges. Oriented to
the Canadian immigration circumstance, but with examples
clearly applicable to the United States as well, the author
provides six strategies for moving from awareness of one's
own nonverbal behaviors (and their possible effects on
others), to creating a classroom atmosphere sufficiently
reassuring to enable students to develop cross-cultural
communication skills.

133. Zamora, Gloria Rodriguez. Nuevo Amanecer/New Dawn (item
        87).

Learning Materials Resources

134. Arora, Ranjit K., and Carlton G. Duncan (Eds.).
        Multicultural Education: Towards Good Practice (item
        88).

135. Banks, James. Teaching Strategies for Ethnic Studies (item
        107).

136. Carter, Dorothy. "Selecting Resources for the Multicultural
      Classroom." Momentum 14 (1) (February 1983): 47-50.

          Presents a series of questions designed to help
      teachers consider their purpose in using particular
      materials and resources as part of their multicultural
      program. The author stresses the importance of relating
      those materials to the ongoing goals and objectives of the
      program, and of making choices that will enhance such
      curriculum emphases as critical literacy skills. The
      article ends with a list of resources including several
      films.

137. Cox, Barbara G., Janet Macauley, and Manuel Ramirez III.
      Neuvas Fronteras/New Frontiers (item 76).

138. Kendall, Frances E. Diversity in the Classroom: A
      Multicultural Approach to the Education of Young
      Children (item 97).

139. Klein, Gillian. Reading into Racism: Bias in Children's
      Literature and Learning Materials. London: Routledge
      and Kegan, 1985.

          An analysis of the many ways in which children's
      literature and learning materials can shape children's
      attitudes about themselves and other people. Criteria for
      selecting materials and ways of developing skills for
      evaluating materials for children are explored, as well as
      strategies for removing bias from the teaching and learning
      experiences. Klein is particularly intriguing in the ways
      she identifies bias appearing in materials across subject
      areas, and in her clarification of underlying issues in
      content presentations that are misleading to the learner.

140. Ramsey, Patricia G. Teaching and Learning in a Diverse
      World: Multicultural Education for Young Children
      (item 83).

141. Saracho, Olivia N., and Bernard Spodek (Eds.).
      Understanding the Multicultural Experience in Early
      Childhood Education (item 125).

142. Tiedt, Pamela L., and Iris M. Tiedt. Multicultural
          Teaching: A Handbook of Activities, Information and
          Resources (item 104).

143. Williams, Leslie R., Yvonne De Gaetano, Charles C.
          Harrington, and Iris R. Sutherland. ALERTA: A
          Multicultural, Bilingual Approach to Teaching Young
          Children (item 85).

CHAPTER IV

MULTICULTURAL TEACHER EDUCATION

Patricia G. Ramsey

History of Multicultural Teacher Education

The incorporation of a multicultural focus into teacher
education began in the 1960s with centers that offered brief
inservice training for teachers in recently desegregated settings.
The formats ranged from one-day workshops to institutes of several
weeks' duration. The topics included intergroup relations,
conflict management, understanding cultural and linguistic
differences, and improving school and community relations.
Training rarely consisted of a comprehensive approach in which all
of these areas were incorporated.
With the inception of Teacher Corps and other federal
programs, the model of a field-based internship was introduced.
Several schools of education began to incorporate community-based
programs in which preservice teachers worked in culturally diverse
communities. These programs, however, were limited to students
who selected them, so that they did not represent a broad reform
in teacher education.
The need for all teachers to be multicultural in their
approach became more appraent in the 1970s. In 1977, the National
Council for the Accreditation of Teacher Education revised its
standards to mandate a multicultural perspective in all teacher
education programs. To support these reforms, several model
teacher preparation programs were funded and implemented, and
there were a number of publications in the late 1970s and early
1980s that provided guidelines and models for the implementation
of the NCATE standards. During this period, programs for
multicultural teacher education were also implemented in other
countries, such as the United Kingdom and Canada.

After the early 1980s, most of the references to
multicultural teacher education have been reviews that criticize
the fragmented and superficial modifications that many teacher
education programs have employed to meet the NCATE standards.
Authors, both here and abroad, point out that there is an
increasing need for a multicultural perspective in all areas of
education, but that little real change has occurred. They
advocate more profound reforms to make teacher education programs
genuinely multicultural.

NCATE Standards for Multicultural Education

Multicultural Education is mandated to be an integral part of
teacher preparation, according to the 1977 standards of the
National Council for the Accreditation of Teacher Education
(NCATE). There are references to multicultural education in
standards on governance, faculty, students, resources, and
long-range planning. The major reference (NCATE, 1977) reads as
follows:

2.1.1 Multicultural Education
Multicultural education is preparation for the social,
political, and economic realities that individuals experience
in culturally diverse and complex human encounters. These
realities have both national and international dimensions.
This preparation provides a process by which an individual
develops competencies for perceiving, believing, evaluating,
and behaving in differential cultural settings. Thus,
multicultural education is viewed as an intervention and an
ongoing assessment process to help institutions and
individuals become more responsive to the human condition,
individual cultural integrity, and cultural pluralism in
society.
Provision should be made for instruction in
multicultural education in teacher education programs.
Multicultural education should receive attention in courses,
seminars, directed readings, laboratory and clinical
experiences, practicum, and other types of field experiences.
Multicultural education could include but not be limited
to the experiences which: (1) promote analytical and
evaluative abilities to confront issues such as participatory
democracy, racism and sexism, and the parity of power; (2)
develop skills for values clarification, including the study
of the manifest and latent transmission of values; (3)
examine the dynamics of diverse cultures and the implications

for developing teaching strategies; and (4) form a basis for
the development of appropriate teaching strategies.
    Standard: **The institution gives evidence of planning
for multicultural education in its teacher education
curricula including both the general and professional studies
components.**

Goals and Guidelines for
Multicultural Teacher Education

    A number of articles and books have articulated the goals of
multicultural teacher education, and several have also provided
guidelines with varying levels of specificity. Most of them
typify Sleeter and Grant's (1987) categories of the human
relations approach and multicultural education, rather than their
category of social reconstructionist.
    Similar to the types of classroom programs reviewed in
Chapter III, the guidelines for teacher education vary in terms of
their focus, breadth, and level of specificity. Banks (1977)
stressed the need for teacher education to foster students'
understanding of multiethnicity and their commitment to a
multicultural perspective. Gay (1977) delineated more specific
attitudinal, cognitive, and skill components of multicultural
teacher education. Bennett (1988) developed a similar model that
includes four areas: (a) knowledge of historical perspectives and
current cultural differences; (b) understandings of culture that
lead to intercultural competence; (c) attitudes that embody a
commitment to reduce racism, prejudice, and discrimination; and
(d) skills in teaching of multicultural students. Using a
competency-based framework, Baptiste and Baptiste (1980)
identified 11 specific multicultural competencies, each with
several related rationales, instructional objectives, enabling
activities, and assessments. In reponse to this last approach,
Grant (1977a) expressed some concerns about whether or not a
multicultural perspective is compatible with the specific
competencies, accountability, and production that characterize
competency-based teacher education. In addition to articles and
books that have focused specifically on teacher education, several
recent books on multicultural educational practices have included
sections or chapters on teacher preparation or the qualifications
of teachers (e.g. Baker, 1983; Banks, 1987a; Ramsey, 1987;
Williams & De Gaetano, 1985).
    The goals and guidelines have addressed a wide range of
topics which fall into the following general categories. First,
writers have stressed the need for prospective and practicing

teachers to monitor their own biases and assumptions, and to have
a clear commitment to present a realistic portrayal of the society
and to approach all children with an enabling attitude (Baker,
1983; Gay, 1977; Ramsey, 1987). Second, authors have addressed
the need to infuse a multicultural perspective into the content of
all liberal arts courses. Banks (1987b) argues that these courses
should be designed to provide students with a meaningful context
for understanding both the lifestyles and life chances of various
ethnic groups. An edited volume by Baskauskas (1986) includes
essays on how to incorporate a multicultural perspective in a
range of college level social science courses. Third, a number of
guidelines offer suggestions on the specific skills that teachers
need in order to successfullly implement a multicultural
perspective in their work. Gay (1983) discusses the need for
prospective teachers to learn how to adapt materials and teacher
styles to be relevant to and effective with a wide range of
children, and to impart a multicultural perspective to all
children. Other writers (e.g., Hayes, 1980) describe skills
specific to effectively communicating with and involving the
community. Kohut (1980) addresses the issue of field experiences,
and ways in which options can be broadened so that students will
have a wider range of experiences.

One goal that is emphasized strongly is the need for teachers
to be skilled at interpreting words, gestures, and behaviors of
people from other cultures, and to be able to convey information
and feelings in ways that are appropriate to specific cultural
groups.   Poor cross-cultural communication skills can create
discomfort, disrupt interactions, and inhibit child-teacher and
family-teacher relationship (Kleifgen, 1987). Mitchell and Watson
(1980) identify several potential sources of cultural conflict
between families and schools, and describe how learning about
family values and lifestyles, individual styles of learning, and
culturally related verbal and nonverbal communication enable
teachers to be more prepared to ease children's transitions into
school. Banks and Benavidez (1980) describe a model of
interpersonal skills training that has been used to prepare
teachers to work with children from a variety of backgrounds.

In addition to educational guidelines, there are a number of
resources on cross-cultural and intercultural communication that
describe techniques for training people to become less
ethnocentric and more sensitive to unfamiliar communication
nuances. These are similar to materials designed for intergroup
education and embody the human relations approach. Sources
include programs designed for international business people, the
military, and foreign service officers. These programs usually
combine information about dimensions of cultural differences, and
experiences such as simulations and role-playing, to help
participants articulate and expand their own perspectives. One

author describes the process as "learning how to learn" (Casse, 1979). With a slightly different approach, a Canadian program uses case studies to help people learn about their reactions to various cross-cultural situations, and to develop strategies for resolving them (Minister of Supply and Services, 1985). Several cross-cultural training programs are included in the annotated bibliography of this chapter.

There are several guidelines on the implementation of multicultural teacher education programs. One of the most comprehensive sources is "Guidelines for Multicultural Teacher Education" by Klassen, Gollnick, and Osayande (1980). The authors describe ways in which institutional governance, curriculum, faculty members, students, and resources should be changed in order to provide an environment supportive of multicultural teaching and learning. Gollnick, Osayande, & Levy (1980) stress community involvement in the planning and development of courses and programs, and the need for the faculty to be both representative of diversity and genuinely committed to a multicultural perspective. Rodriguez (1983) describes a faculty development program which is designed to facilitate the implementation of multicultural teacher education at the individual and institutional levels. The need to recruit and retain students from more diverse backgrounds is emphasized in Grant, Sabol, & Sleeter's (1980) article. They describe changes in recruitment, admissions, retention, and post-graduate placement policies that need to be made in order to meet this goal.

Case Studies of Teacher Education Programs

Several case studies of program in the United States and in the United Kingdom illustrate ways in which teacher education can be changed to incorporate a multicultural perspective effectively. These accounts also provide insights into some of the problems that impede these reforms, or render programs ineffective and/or short-lived.

In their edited volume, Klassen and Gollnick (1977) included case studies of the implementation of a multicultural perspective in six teacher education programs. Five of the programs were at large public universities, and one was a regional center established to assist schools with problems related to desegregation. All of these programs were comprehensive and offered models of training that addressed the goals and guidelines described above. Each description includes a brief account of the history of the program, the clients that it served, and a projection of the future growth and directions of the program.

Some of the studies include descriptions of problems that had been encountered in the establishment of these programs.

In Gollnick et al.'s volume (1980) prepared for the American Association of Colleges for Teacher Education, 13 case studies are presented. These programs were selected because they were considered exemplary and represented a variety of institutions, ranging from small private colleges to large state universities. Each case study includes descriptions of the institution, curricula, governance, faculty and students, and projections about the future strength and direction of the program.

According to the authors, each of these programs addressed the NCATE goals, although there was some variation in the extent to which they had integrated multicultural perspective throughout their programs (Gollnick et al., 1980). Interestingly, they concluded that small colleges were more successful in integrating multicultural education throughout the institution. Large universities, while often having more resources and grants, were less flexible and had less involvement of the total faculty.

The authors felt that there were many strengths in these programs. First, they were supported by the ethnic communities and local education agencies with whom they worked. In terms of funding, most of the programs were initiated and maintained with "hard" monies from the institution. Almost all of the programs included field experiences and student teaching placements in culturally diverse settings. Administrative support for multicultural programs was also evident in the active recruitment of minority faculty, and in faculty development programs that supported individuals' efforts to develop skills in related areas and to conduct research and consulting projects in culturally diverse communities. Finally, all the programs enjoyed the enthusiastic support of their students.

The weaknesses that the authors identified suggested that a multicultural perspective had not yet been fully embraced by the institutions. First, few of the institutions had faculties and student bodies that represented the ethnic/racial diversity of this country. Second, the multicultural programs were usually adjunct, rather than fully integrated into the core of the teacher education programs. Third, some administrators and faculty viewed multicultural education as a fad that would soon disappear, and did not give it serious attention. Related to this, programs were often dependent on a few dedicated individuals who were potentially jeopardizing their careers due to the amount of time they were spending in promoting and sustaining these programs. Finally, both short- and long-range plans seemed vague and did not use the needs assessments and evaluation procedures that were available. The authors concluded that there is a great need for research to assess what aspects of programs are most effective, and to determine the effect of these programs on teachers and students.

One institution in England that has worked to meet many of the goals addressed previously is the program at Bradford College in Sunderland Polytechnic Institute in England (Lynch, 1981). A case study of how this perspective was implemented at Bradford College (Arora, 1986) illustrates the profound changes that must occur in the institutional structure as well as in the content of courses, in order to offer training that is authentically multicultural.

The depth of thinking and deliberation that is required to mount a truly multicultural program is illustrated by a description of the process one institution underwent to design a single course for students who were going to teach Native American children (Mathieu, 1978). During the planning period, the political and academic ramifications of the course created tensions between members of different disciplines and constituents that were resolved only after protracted deliberations.

Reviews of Multicultural Teacher Education

Evaluations of Programs

The reviews of multicultural teacher education programs have been few in number and have reported rather discouraging findings. Recent articles have advocated a comprehensive, indepth approach that is infused in all aspects of teacher education (Gay, 1983; Grant, 1983; Sims, 1983). However, in a small survey reported by Olstad, Foster, & Wyman in 1983, most institutions used only course work to meet the NCATE requirements. There were three ways in which this coursework was structured: (1) a single course that is required of all certification candidates, (2) electives from a list of approved courses, or (3) components in existng courses. Several articles criticize simplistic approaches that involve adding only one or two courses, because multicultural education is simply appended to the exisiting curriculum, rather than being integrated throughout the whole program (Olstad et al., 1983; Sims, 1983). In a longitudinal study, Bennett (1988) found that, although the base-line multicultural course had a positive impact on the students' teaching behaviors, there was not follow-up instruction in multicultural education in subsequent courses or student teaching. She also pointed out that, given the range of readiness levels with which students enter the course, individualized experiences may be needed in order to have an impact on all teacher education students. Even in a fairly

comprehensive program in which multicultural education was
incorporated in a number of courses, Grant (1981) found that there
was a tendency for course instructors to repeatedly cover the same
"safe" ground, such as identifying bias in text books, and to
avoid engaging students in authentically implementaing a
multicultural perspective. In a follow-up study, Grant and
Koskela (1986) found that the quality of the course information
had improved in that students were exposed to a greater variety of
multicultural concepts, but that very little attention was given
to the application and integration of multicultural perspectives
in the classroom. The authors emphasize the need for students to
see teachers modeling the implementation of multicultural
education. Another problem in many schools of education is that
faculty have little commitment to multicultural education. A
survey of faculty attitudes (Wayson, 1988) revealed that
professors had little interest in incorporating a multicultural
perspective in their courses because they had neither the
motivation nor the knowledge to do it.

     Similar criticisms have been articulated by authors in the
United Kingdom. In a recent critique of the British teacher
education programs, Lynch (1986) decries the failure of teacher
education to fully embrace a multicultural perspective. He points
out that there are still very few minority faculty members or
leaders in the teacher education field, and prescribes staff
development for all teacher educators so they will be more
committed and more skilled at teaching from a multicultural
perspective. He is adamant that these changes must occur on
institutional and national levels in order to make teacher
education in Britain truly multicultural. Nixon (1985) expresses
similar criticisms of British teacher education, and emphasizes
the negative impact of insecurity in most teacher education
programs, due to shifting government policies and uncertain
resources, on the development of long-term and effective programs.
Like Lynch, he notes that the teaching profession and its
leadership is still primarily white, and attributes this
intransigence to the reluctance of educators at all levels to
share their power with members of other groups. He also discusses
the cynicism and evasiveness of many teacher educators, who
dismiss the importance of multicultural education as a fad.
Watson (1984) attributes the persistence of ethnocentrism in
British education to the conservatism of the current government
and the failure of teacher education programs to provide either
inservice or preservice training that effectively changes teacher
attitudes.

Assessment of Teacher Education Students

There have been relatively few studies of the effects of teacher education programs on students attitudes, skills, and knowledge, and those that have been done present a mixed picture. Many students are positively affected by multicultural modules in courses (e.g. Heninger, 1981), but a sizeable minority is not. Furthermore, there is evidence that the effects are short-lived and are not supported by adequate skills and knowledge that enable students to implement multicultural education. One recent study (Bennett, 1988) showed that exposure to multicultural education had a positive effect on students, but was most effective with students who were open-minded at the outset of the course. Furthermore, without any subsequent instruction, the initial knowledge and attitude gains were not maintained at the post-test level one year later. In a large study of student teacher attitudes (Moultry, 1988; Wayson, 1988), the majority of the respondents (60-70%) expressed some awareness of issues related to diversity, and had considerable empathy and concern for groups that have suffered discrimination. However, 30 - 40% showed the opposite pattern. A little over one-half of the students indicated that they felt confident to teach in a multicultural classroom, whereas the remainder did not. Furthermore, there was only moderate interest in teaching in multicultural settings. Very few of the respondents know elementary facts about the history, culture, and contribution of ethnic groups they are most likely to encounter in American schools. Thus, even if they wanted to broaden their curriculum, they did not have the knowledge to support these efforts.

There are very few studies that have followed up graduates of multicultural teacher education programs, so the long-term effectiveness of these programs has not been evaluated. In one study (Aotaki-Phenice & Kostelnik, 1983), preservice and graduate students in an early childhood teacher preparation program were compared. While both groups supported multicultural education, there was no significant difference in their attitudes, which raises questions about the impact of their training experiences. While the effect on individuals may not be clear, participation in a multicultural program appears to substantially improve preservice teachers' employment prospects (Mahan & Lacefield, 1982). In this study of 733 graduates of a teacher preparation program, those students who had taught in culturally diverse settings had a consistently higher chance of finding the type of teaching job that they wanted.

Assessment Instruments

     There are a number of instruments that have been used to
measure student attitudes. Because researchers have adapted
existing instruments or have created their own, most of them are
not in print, but could be obtained by contacting specific
authors. Bennett (1988) used a revised Social Distance Scale to
measure students' reactions to members of 30 ethnic groups. She
also developed a thirty item Multicultural Knowledge Test which
uses true and false questions to determine the level of students'
knowledge about other groups. A modified version of the Zeigler
scale (1980) was used to assess Openness to Human Diversity. With
23 Lickert scale type items, the test measured levels of
receptiveness to diverse groups, reactions to equity policies, and
opinions about interracial couples. Moultry (1988) and Wayson
(1988) developed The Multicultural Teaching Scale from several
sources including Grant (1977b), Halverson (1975), Noar (1974),
and the State of California (1977). Cross-cultural programs often
include assessment of knowledge, perception, and attitude change
to measure the effectiveness of the training (e.g. Renwick, 1980)
that also might be adapted to measure both the short and long-term
impact of multicultural programs.
     In terms of assessing programmatic change, this review of the
literature revealed only one instrument designed specifically for
that purpose. Klassen, Gollnick, and Osayande (1980) include
specific questions to use in evaluations of teacher education
programs.

Preservice and Inservice Programs

     Most program guidelines, descriptions, and critiques do not
make a clear distinction between preservice and inservice
training, with the exception of a few of the case studies. The
implementation of a multicultural perspective does, however, face
different challenges in the two types of programs.
     Undergraduate preservice programs include four years of
college, which allow time for students to be exposed to a
multicultural perspective in many different ways. With this
comprehensive approach, there is more potential to effect
attitudinal change. Furthermore, undergraduate students are less
likely to have acquired fixed or cynical ideas about particular
groups. At the same time, undergraduates are often very anxious
about their own teaching skills, and this self-preoccupation makes
it difficult for them to think about broader educational issues or
address the needs of other groups.
     Recent calls for reform of teacher education, in particular
the Holmes report, are advocating that all teacher education be
done at the graduate level. While this type of program has the

advantage that students are more mature and have a solid liberal arts background, this format does reduce the amount of time that students can be exposed to the concept of multicultural education. In particular, they are likely to have completed their liberal arts program with little awareness of the need to have a broad base of cultural literacy in order to be effective teachers.

Inservice training of practicing teachers poses some particular challenges, because it is frequently done in single sessions, with a number of different instructors. This structure often results in a fragmented and incomplete experience (Nixon, 1985) and makes it difficult for participants to honestly and thoroughly explore their own attitudes and to have experiences that challenge them. Even graduate courses, which have more continuity, often meet only once a week late in the afternoon and evening, and are therefore less conducive to extended discussion. Furthermore, inservice training often does not provide a vehicle for teachers to grapple with the challenges posed by their particular situations, so teachers feel frustrated. Because teachers are often in situations that they themselves cannot change, inservice sessions may only focus on surface issues rather than on the roots of some difficulties. Dunn (1986) describes some of the problems with implementing effective inservice programs in England. On the positive side, practicing teachers enter the training with more experience and fewer "survival" concerns that characterize preservice students. Thus, practicing teachers may be able to make more immediate use of the available training (Baker, 1983).

While the goals of multicultural teacher education are the same for undergraduate and graduate preservice teachers and for inservice participants, the ways in which they are implemented must take into account the specific needs, experiences, and strengths of the students.

Summary

There are a number of resources to guide teacher educators in the task of making their programs multicultural. Guidelines, case studies, and commentaries provide detailed descriptions of goals, methods, and potential problems. Unfortunately, there is little research on the effectiveness of various models, so that setting priorities and gaining support for the necessary funding and staffing are difficult tasks. In the very recent literature, however, there are signs that the effect of multicultural teacher education is beginning to be studied in a more systematic way.

The tone of the writings has changed over the past decade. In the late 1970s there was a proliferation of materials that enthusiastically predicted that teacher education would become multicultural. After the early 1980s, the tone is more critical, as teacher educators recognize the difficulty of making meaningful changes in their institutions. The British critiques show some evidence of moving multicultural teacher education toward the social reconstructionist perspective that is advocated by Sleeter and Grant (1987). As with multicultural education as a whole, the youthful enthusiasm for the reform of teacher education that prevailed in the 1970s has become the critical and thoughtful analysis of the 1980s.

Three positive indicators relieve this otherwise grim outlook for multicultural teacher education. First, the more recent writings recognize the depth and subtlety of the personal, institutional, and societal changes required to make schools truly multicultural, which may lead to more thoughtful and effective approaches. Second, these efforts are international in scope, and the exchange and collaboration among teacher educators in several countries has the potential to enrich and accelerate the reform of teacher education. Third, many colleges and universities, alarmed at the increase in racism among their students, are initiating efforts to incorporate a multicultural focus in their liberal arts curricula. If successful, these reforms will support the goals of multicultural teacher education.

References

Aotaki-Phenice, L., and Marjorie Kostelnik. "Attitudes of Early
Childhood Educators on Multicultural/ Multiethnic Education."
Journal of Multilingual and Multicultural Development 4
(1983): 41-46.

Arora, Ranjit. "Initial Teacher Training (A Case Study of a
Decade of Change in Bradford)." Multicultural Education:
Towards Good Practice. Edited by Ranjit Arora and Carlton
Duncan. London, England: Routledge & Kegan, 1986, pp.
161-81.

Baker, Gwendolyn. Planning and Organizing for Multicultural
Instruction. Reading, MA: Addison-Wesley, 1983.

Banks, George P., and Patricia L. Benavidez. "Interpersonal
Skills Training in Multicultural Education." Multicultural
Teacher Education: Preparing Educators to Provide
Educational Equity. Edited by H. Prentice Baptiste, Mira L.
Baptiste, and Donna M. Gollnick. Washington, DC: American
Association of Colleges for Teacher Education, 1980, pp.
177-201.

Banks, James A. "The Implications of Multicultural Education for
Teacher Education." Pluralism and the American Teacher.
Edited by Frank H. Klassen and Donna M. Gollnick.
Washington, DC: American Association of Colleges for Teacher
Education, 1977, pp. 1-30.

Banks, James A. Multiethnic Education: Theory and Practice.
Boston, MA: Allyn & Bacon, Inc., 1987.

Banks, James A. "The Social Studies, Ethnic Diversity, and Social
Change." Elementary School Journal 87 (1987): 531-42.

Baptiste, Mira L., and H. Prentice Baptiste. "Competencies toward
Multiculturalism." Multicultural Teacher Education:
Preparing Educators to Provide Educational Equity. Edited

by H. Prentice Baptiste, Mira L. Baptiste, and Donna M. Gollnick. Washington, DC: American Association of Colleges for Teacher Education, 1980, pp. 44-72.

Baskauskas, Liucija. (Ed.). Unmasking Culture: Cross-Cultural Perspectives in Social and Behavioral Sciences. Novato, CA: Chandler & Charp, 1986.

Bennett Christine I. "The Effects of a Multicultural Education Course on Preservice Teachers' Attitudes, Knowledge and Behavior." Paper presented at the Annual Meeting of the American Research Association in New Orleans, April, 1988.

Bowles, Samuel, and Herbert Gintis. Schooling in Capitalist America: Educational Reform and the Contradictions of Economic Life. New York: Basic Books, 1976.

California State Department of Education, Office of Intergroup Relations. "Guide for Multicultural Education: Content and Context." Sacramento, CA: 1977.

Casse, Pierre. Training for the Cross-Cultural Mind. Washington, DC: The Society for Intercultural Education, Training and Research, 1979.

Dunn, Dave. "In-service Mis-education." Multicultural Education: Towards Good Practice. Edited by Ranjit Arora and Carlton Duncan. London, England: Routledge & Kegan, 1986, pp. 182-99.

Gay, Geneva. "Curriculum for Multicultural Teacher Education." Pluralism and the American Teacher. Edited by Frank H. Klassen and Donna M. Gollnick. Washington, DC: American Association of Colleges for Teacher Education, 1977, pp. 31-62.

Gentemann, Karen M., and Tony L. Whitehead. "The Cultural Broker Concept in Bicultural Education." Journal of Negro Education 52 (1983): 118-29.

Gollnick, Donna M., Kobla I.M. Osayande, and Jack Levy. Multicultural Teacher Education: Case Studies of Thirteen Programs. Washington, DC: American Association of Colleges for Teacher Education, 1980.

Grant, Carl A. "Education That Is Multicultural and P/CBTE: Discussion and Recommendations for Teacher Education." Pluralism and the American Teacher. Edited by Frank H.

Klassen and Donna M. Gollnick. Washington, DC: American Association of Colleges for Teacher Education, 1977a, pp. 63-80.

Grant, Carl A. "Education That Is Multicultural and Teacher Preparation: An Examination from the Perspectives of Preservice Students." Journal of Educational Research 75 (1981): 95-101.

Grant, Carl A. (Ed.). "Multicultural Teacher Education: Commitments, Issues and Applications." Washington, DC: Association for Supervision and Curriculum Development, 1977b.

Grant, Carl A. (Ed.). "Multicultural Teacher Education - Renewing the Discussion: A Response to Martin Haberman." Journal of Teacher Education 34 (March-April 1983): 29-32.

Grant, Carl A., and Ruth A. Koskela. "Education That Is Multicultural and the Relationship Between Preservice Campus Learning and Field Experiences." Journal of Educational Research 79 (1986): 197-204.

Grant, Carl A., Ruth Sabol, and Christine E. Sleeter. "Recruitment, Admissions, Retention, and Placement for Educational Equity: An Analysis of the Process." Multicultural Teacher Education: Preparing Educators to Provide Educational Equity. Edited by H. Prentice Baptiste, Mira L. Baptiste, and Donna M. Gollnick. Washington, DC: American Association of Colleges for Teacher Education, 1980, pp. 7-43.

Halverson, Claire, B. "Checking Your Schools for Cultural Pluralism." Evanston, IL: National College of Education, Center for Program Development in Equal Educational Opportunity.

Hayes, Susanna. "The Community and Teacher Education." Multicultural Teacher Education: Preparing Educators to Provide Educational Equity. Edited by H. Prentice Baptiste, Mira L. Baptiste, and Donna M. Gollnick. Washington, DC: American Association of Colleges for Teacher Education, 1980, pp. 94-108.

Klassen, Frank H., and Donna M. Gollnick (Eds.). Pluralism and the American Teacher. Washington, DC: American Association of Colleges for Teacher Education, 1977.

Klassen, Frank H., Donna M. Gollnick, and Kobla I.M. Osayande.
    Multicultural Teacher Education: Guidelines for
    Implementation, volume four. Washington, DC: American
    Association of Colleges for Teacher Education, 1980.

Kleifgen, Jo Ann. "What can be Learned from Student- Teachers'
    Cross-Cultural Communicative Failures?" Paper presented at
    the annual meeting of the American Educational Research
    Association, Washington, DC: April, 1987.

Kohut, Sylvester. "Field Experiences in Preservice Professional
    Studies." Multicultural Teacher Education: Preparing
    Educators to Provide Educational Equity. Edited by H.
    Prentice Baptiste, Mira L. Baptiste, and Donna M. Gollnick.
    Washington, DC: American Association of Colleges for Teacher
    Education, 1980, 73-93.

Luke, Allan. "Linguistic Stereotypes, the Divergent Speaker and
    the Teaching of Literacy." Journal of Curriculum Studies 18
    (1986): 397-408.

Lynch, James. "An Initial Typology of Perspectives on Staff
    Development for Multicultural Teacher Education."
    Multicultural Education: The Interminable Debate. Edited by
    Sohan Modgil, Gajendra K. Verma, Kanka Mallick, and Celia
    Modgil. London: The Falmer Press, 1986, pp. 149-65.

Lynch, James. "Multicultural Education and the Training of
    Teachers: A Case Study." The South Pacific Journal of
    Teacher Education 9 (April 1981): 43-54.

Mahan, James M., and Warren Lacefield. "Employability and
    Multi-Cultural Teacher Preparation." Educational Research
    Quarterly 7 (1982): 15-20.

Mathieu, David J. "Adoption and Development of Teacher
    Certification Requirement." Journal of American Indian
    Education 18 (October 1978): 17-22.

Minister of Supply and Services. Cross-Cultural Awareness
    Education and Training for Professionals: A Manual.
    Edmonton, Alberta: Department of Education, 1985.

Mitchell, Edna, and Marilyn Watson. "Personal Cultural
    Orientations and Educational Practices." Multicultural
    Teacher Education: Preparing Educators to Provide
    Educational Equity. Edited by H. Prentice Baptiste, Mira L.

Baptiste, and Donna M. Gollnick. Washington, DC: American Association of Colleges for Teacher Education, 1980, pp. 154-76.

Moultry, Murphy. "Multicultural Education Among Seniors in the College of Education at Ohio State University." Paper presented at the Annual Meeting of the American Educational Research Association in New Orleans, April, 1988.

National Council for Accreditation of Teacher Education. Standards for the Accreditation of Teacher Education. Washington, DC, 1977.

Nixon, Jon. "Teacher Education." A Teacher's Guide to Multicultural Education. New York: Basil Blackwell, 1985, pp. 152-69.

Noar, Gertrude. "The Teacher and Integration." Washington, DC: National Education Association, 1974.

Olstad, R. G., Clifford D. Foster, and Richard M. Wyman. "Multicultural Education for Preservice Teachers." Integrated Education 21 (1983): 137-39.

Ramsey, Patricia G. Teaching and Learning in a Diverse World: Multicultural Education for Young Children. New York: Teachers College Press, 1987.

Renwick, George W. Evaluation Handbook for Cross-Cultural Training and Multicultural Education. LaGrange Park, IL: Intercultural Network, Inc., 1980.

Rodriguez, Fred. Mainstreaming a Multicultural Concept into Teacher Education: Guidelines for Teacher Training. Saratoga, CA: R & E Publishers, 1983.

Saracho, Olivia N., and Bernard Spodek. "Preparing Teachers for Multicultural Classrooms." Understanding the Multicultural Experience in Early Childhood Education. Edited by Olivia Saracho and Bernard Spodek. Washington, DC: National Association for the Education of Young Children, 1983, pp.125-46.

Sims, William E. "Preparing Teachers for Multicultural Classrooms." Momentum 14 (February 1983): 42-44.

Sleeter, Christine E., and Carl A. Grant. "An Analysis of Multicultural Education in the United States." Harvard Educational Review 57 (November 1987): 421-44.

Watson, Keith. "Training Teachers in the United Kingdom for a
    Multicultural Society - The Rhetoric and the Reality."
    Journal of Multilingual and Multicultural Development 5
    (1984): 385-400.

Wayson, William W. "Multicultural Education Among Seniors in the
    College of Education at Ohio State University." Paper
    presented at the Annual Meeting of the American Educational
    Research Association in New Orleans, April, 1988.

Williams, Leslie R., Yvonne De Gaetano, Iris R. Sutherland and
    Charles C. Harrington. ALERTA: A Multicultural, Bilingual
    Approach to Teaching Young Children. Reading, MA:
    Addison-Wesley, 1985.

Zeigler, Susan. "Measuring Inter-Ethnic Attitudes in a
    Multi-Ethnic Context." Canadian Ethnic Studies III(3),
    (1980): 43-55.

Bibliography

144. Arora, Ranjit. "Initial Teacher Training (A Case Study of a Decade of Change in Bradford)." Multicultural Education: Towards Good Practice. Edited by Ranjit Arora and Carlton Duncan. London, England: Routledge & Kegan, 1986, pp. 161-81.

This case study describes the process and sequence of events by which the teacher training program at Bradford College in England was changed to reflect a more multicultural focus. (For more information about this program, see the annotation under Lynch, 1981 ANNOT. 173) The author details the external factors that facilitated this implementation, that included the merging of the teacher training program with the community studies program, and the location of the school in an ethnically diverse area. Implementation involved changes in admisssion procedures, administrative structures, liaisons with the local schools, course content, and staffing policy. The extent of changes illustrates well the kind of profound restructuring that must occur for programs to truly become multicultural, in fact as well as intent.

145. Baker, Gwendolyn. Planning and Organizing for Multicultural Instruction. Reading, MA: Addison-Wesley, 1983, pp. 41-62.

In this chapter the author describes a model of teacher training that includes three phases: first, the acquisition of information about one's own cultural identity and other cultures; second, the development of a philosophy that embodies a commitment to multicultural education; and third, the involvement in the implementation of multicultural instruction. The chapter concludes with ten imperatives for teacher training programs.

146. Banks, George P., and Patricia L. Benavidez. "Interpersonal
          Skills Training in Multicultural Education."
          Multicultural Teacher Education: Preparing Educators
          to Provide Educational Equity. Edited by H. Prentice
          Baptiste, Mira L. Baptiste, and Donna M. Gollnick.
          Washington, DC: American Association of Colleges for
          Teacher Education, 1980, pp. 177-201.

          This model of training seeks to improve teachers'
      effectiveness by increasing the quantity and quality of
      their interpersonal responses. The authors review studies
      that have found that teachers often react differentially to
      children from diverse backgrounds, and describe how teachers
      can become more effective with a broader range of students
      if they increase their interpersonal awaremess and skills.
      In contrast to the more conceptual approach of human
      relations training, this model provides specific skills in
      attending, responding, personalizing, and initiating with
      students. The authors discuss how this model can be
      integrated into a multicultural framework, and describe
      training procedures and models for delivery in higher
      education and in service training.

147. Banks, James A. "The Implications of Multicultural
          Education for Teacher Education." Pluralism and the
          American Teacher. Edited by Frank H. Klassen and Donna
          M. Gollnick. Washington, DC: American Association of
          Colleges for Teacher Education, 1977, pp. 1-30.

          In this chapter, Banks discusses the distinctions among
      multicultural education, ethnic studies, and multiethnic
      education. He briefly reviews the research on teacher
      attitudes, and delineates and critiques the assimilationist,
      pluralist, and pluralist- assimilationist ideologies. The
      chapter concludes with a discussion of the five stages of
      emerging ethnic encapsulation, ethnic identity, biethnicity,
      and multiethnicity and the curricular implications of each
      stage in teacher education programs.

148. Baptiste, Mira L., and H. Prentice Baptiste. "Competencies
          toward Multiculturalism." Multicultural Teacher
          Education: Preparing Educators to Provide Educational
          Equity. Edited by H. Prentice Baptiste, Mira L.
          Baptiste, and Donna M. Gollnick. Washington, DC:
          American Association of Colleges for Teacher Education,
          1980, pp. 44-72.

The authors summarize the history of various delivery
systems and techniques for training teachers to become more
multicultural in their approach. They then describe in
detail how the goals of multicultural teaching can be met by
using the framework of competency-based teacher education,
and argue that the specification of skills and the emphasis
on mastery ensure a more systematic approach in
multicultural teacher education. The authors articulate 11
competencies divided into three phases: cultural pluralism,
multicultural education, and multiculturalism. For each
competency the authors include a rationale, instructional
objectives, illustrative enabling activities, methods of
assessing the mastery of that competency, and a list of
suggested courses that potentially lead to mastery.

149. Baskauskas, Liucija   (Ed.). Unmasking Culture:
       Cross-Cultural Perspectives in Social and Behavioral
       Sciences. Novato, CA: Chandler & Charp, 1986.

This edited volume includes seven essays on how to
teach history, sociology, psychology, and geography from a
multicultural perspective. The authors challenge the notion
that many of these areas are, by definition, multicultural,
and point out ways in which a pro-Western bias is embodied
in the basic theories and structures of these fields. Each
chapter includes a list of bibliographic and media resources
that college faculty could use in their courses. Several
chapters also include sample syllabi and/or examples of
class discussions and activities.

150. Brislin, Richard W., and Paul Pederson. Cross- Cultural
       Orientation Programs. New York: Gardner Press, 1976.

This volume describes a variety of cross- cultural
orientation programs and reviews the ways in which they have
been used in a number of settings. The book also discusses
the types of audiences for these programs (e.g.
multinational companies, government agencies, etc.) and
provides guidelines for evaluating the effective- ness of
these programs.

151. Casse, Pierre. Training for the Cross-Cultural Mind.
       Washington, DC: The Society for Intercultural
       Education, Training, and Research, 1979.

This handbook provides very specific exercises and
techniques for conducting workshops in cross-cultural
awareness and communication. The 15 workshops involve
participants in studies and experiences related to the
different aspects of culture, cross-cultural communications,
and adaptations to new cultures. Many of the techniques and
exercises can be used in teacher preparation courses.

152. Craft, Maurice (Ed.). Teaching in a Multicultural Society:
      The Task for Teacher Education. Sussex, England: The
      Falmer Press, 1981.

      Papers presented at a seminar in England in 1981
articulate some of the current problems in implementing
multicultural teacher education. The discussions highlight
the need for more leadership, more clearly articulated
curriculum goals, more dialogue about these issues, and more
expertise in this area of education. Presenters report on
the present status and needs of both preservice and in
service training, and set goals for action at both the local
and national levels. Each series of reports is followed by
a discussion that summarizes the major points raised by
participants in responses to the papers.

153. Gay, Geneva. "Curriculum for Multicultural Teacher
      Education." Pluralism and the American Teacher.
      Edited by Frank H. Klassen and Donna M. Gollnick.
      Washington, DC: American Association of Colleges for
      Teacher Education, 1977, pp. 31-62.

      In this chapter, Gay articulates the three curriculum
components of multicultural teacher education. The first is
the knowledge component, which includes the content of
cultural pluralism (information about the historical and
contemporary experiences and contributions of diverse
groups), the understanding of the philosophy of
multicultural education, the awareness and interpretation of
classroom dynamics especially in relationship to ethnic
differences among children or between children and teachers,
and information about ethnic materials. Second, the
attitudes component embodies realistic attitudes toward
cultural diversity, enabling attitudes toward all children
from all backgrounds, awareness of one's own attitudes, and
a sense of security about teaching about ethnic diversity.
Third, the skills component includes cross-cultural
interactional skills, the ability to critique and select

multicultural curriculum materials, and the skills to incorporate a wide range of cultures into the curriculum through a variety of methods and materials.

154. Gay, Geneva. "Why Multicultural Education in Teacher Preparation Programs?" Contemporary Education 54 (1983): 79-85.

The author argues that a multicultural perspective is essential for all teachers for a variety of legal, social, pedagogical, and psychological reasons. Teachers who are open to diversity and knowledgeable about ethnic differences are prepared to teach children from a variety of backgrounds. Gay states that little progress has been made to date on extending the data bases of sociology and psychology to include ethnicity in a constructive way. She argues that preservice teachers need to learn more about the wide range of possibilities in human behavior, and that all teacher education courses must reflect a multicultural perspective.

155. Gentemann, Karen M., and Tony L. Whitehead. "The Cultural Broker Concept in Bicultural Education." Journal of Negro Education 52 (1983): 118-29.

Although this article describes a model in which college students were trained to be cultural brokers for their "highrisk" peers from low income backgrounds, it is applicable to teacher education, as it describes a crucial role of teachers who work with children from backgrounds that differ from the culture of schools. Cultural brokers translate the academic subculture to students who are unfamiliar with it and assist them in negotiating the system, as well as facilitating adaptations on the part of the institution to be more responsive to the high-risk students. They also serve as role models, as they demonstrate the ability to negotiate both cultures. This model emphasizes the reciprocal nature of the adjustment between students and classrooms, rather than the one-way conformity often required by schools. The inclusion of this training in teacher preparation programs provides teachers with a clearer understanding of the adjustments that many children need to make, and gives teachers concrete means to facilitate this process for both students and schools.

156. Gollnick, Donna M., Kobla I.M. Osayande, and Jack Levy.
      Multicultural Teacher Education: Case Studies of
      Thirteen Programs, Volume Two. Washington, DC:
      American Association of Colleges for Teacher Education,
      1980.

      This series of case studies describes a range of
      teacher preparation programs at institutions ranging from
      small private colleges to large state universities. Each
      account includes a description of the institution, the
      composition of students and faculty, a detailed description
      of the curricula at undergraduate and, where appropriate,
      graduate levels, resources available, and future directions
      of the program. The authors summarize the overall strengths
      and weaknesses of the programs in the final chapter.

157. Grant, Carl A. "Education That Is Multicultural and P/CBTE:
      Discussion and Recommendations for Teacher Education."
      Pluralism and the American Teacher. Edited by Frank H.
      Klassen and Donna M. Gollnick. Washington, DC:
      American Association of Colleges for Teacher Education,
      1977a, pp. 63-80.

      In this chapter, Grant raises some questions about the
      compatibility of competency based teacher education and
      multicultural education. Of particular concern are the
      fragmentation of the teaching act into discrete skills, the
      reliance on specific and concrete objectives, and uniformity
      of criteria for competence, all of which may contradict the
      complexity, diversity, and flexibility that are inherent in
      a multicultural perspective. He states that the emphasis on
      self-evaluation and self-pacing is congruent with the goals
      of multicultural teacher preparation, but expresses concern
      that the specificity of the objectives may not allow
      prospective teachers to respond and grow as unique
      individuals within their own cultural orientations. He
      concludes by listing recommendations for all programs of
      teacher education, including those with a competency- based
      orientation. These include a faculty committed to
      multicultural education, practical experiences with people
      of diverse cultures, courses that teach the difference
      between diversity and deficiency, instructional materials
      that reflect cultural diversity, and innovative methods of
      research to study the effectiveness of programs.

158. Grant, Carl A. "Education That Is Multicultural and Teacher
      Preparation: An Examination from the Perspectives of
      Preservice Students." Journal of Educational Research
      75 (1981): 95-101.

In this study, 17 students who had received baseline instruction in multicultural education were interviewed at the end of each of the three remaining semesters in their teacher education program. Results showed that, while the majority of students had received some additional instruction in multicultural education, the content was limited to discussions of bias in materials, and problems of racism in schools and society. Only a small number of students received any additional instruction during their practicum, and only four students attempted to apply these concepts in their own teaching. Students appeared to be concerned about increasing their own awareness and applying these principles only if they were ordered or encouraged to do so by school or university personnel. Grant argues that an intensive introduction to multicultural education is insufficient, that this perspective needs to be infused at all levels of teacher preparation, and that students should be placed in classrooms that will expand their understanding of human diversity.

159. Grant, Carl A. (Ed.). "Multicultural Teacher Education: Commitments, Issues and Applications." Washington, DC: Association for Supervision and Curriculum Development, 1977b.

In this position paper, Carl Grant argues that Haberman's statement that teacher educators need to provide students with more specific multicultural teaching skills is insufficient. According to Grant, students must first have experiences that help them to develop a philosophy so that they are motivated to implement a multicultural perspective, regardless of the priorities in their schools. Second, students need experiences throughout their teacher education programs that actively involve them in the implementation of this perspective, so that they gain both confidence and commitment to actively engage in this process.

160. Grant, Carl A. (Ed.). "Multicultural Teacher Education - Renewing the Discussion: A Response to Martin Haberman." Journal of Teacher Education 34 (March-April 1983): 29-32.

In this study, 23 students in an elementary teacher
education program were followed through their elementary
preservice program. They were interviewed before and after
their student teaching semesters, and some were observed
during their student teaching. Although there was evidence
that the students gained some multicultural knowledge from
their courses, they applied very little of it in their
classrooms during student teaching. The authors attribute
this failure to the fact that the courses did not emphasize
practical applications enough, and to the lack of models of
good multicultural teaching in the schools.

161. Grant, Carl A., Ruth Sabol, and Christine E. Sleeter.
       "Recruitment, Admissions, Retention, and Placement for
       Educational Equity: An Analysis of the Process."
       Multicultural Teacher Education: Preparing Educators
       to Provide Educational Equity. Edited by H. Prentice
       Baptiste, Mira L. Baptiste, and Donna M. Gollnick.
       Washington, DC: American Association of Colleges for
       Teacher Education, 1980, pp. 7-43.

       The authors discuss enrollment patterns of
nontraditional students by analyzing the existing patterns
and the related issues in each of the following phases:
recruitment, admissions, retention, and postgraduate
placement. They include specific information on enrollment
trends and detailed recommendations for policies and
procedures for each of these components.

162. Grove, Cornelius Lee. Communications Across Cultures.
       Washington, DC: National Education Association, 1976.

       This monograph briefly describes some of the problems
that can occur in cross-cultural communication and analyzes
them from both psychological and anthropological
perspectives. The author concludes with a review of a few
cross-cultural studies that illustrate cultural differences
in communication and thought patterns.

163. Hayes, Susanna. "The Community and Teacher Education."
       Multicultural Teacher Education: Preparing Educators
       to Provide Educational Equity. Edited by H. Prentice
       Baptiste, Mira L. Baptiste, and Donna M. Gollnick.
       Washington, DC: American Association of Colleges for
       Teacher Education, 1980, pp. 94-108.

The main thesis of this chapter is that the education of teachers should be the shared responsibility of the educational institution and the communities that will employ the teachers. Parent and lay groups can advise teacher educators on the types of skills that students need to effectively communicate with members of the community, and the kinds of information that they need to work effectively with the children of that locale. Congruent with the goals and guidelines described previously, the author suggests that students have a variety of contacts and field experiences in order to learn about the subtle ways in which people in the community interact. Parents, community people, and practicing teachers might be involved as adjunct faculty to provide some of this training.

164.   Henington, Mack. "Effect of Intensive Multicultural, Non-Sexist Instruction on Secondary Student Teachers." Educational Research Quarterly 6 (1981): 65-75.

Using an experimental design, the author compared the student knowledge and attitudes before and after an intensive series of classes and experiences related to multicultural non-sexist education. Results indicated that the students who had these experiences made significant knowledge and attitudinal gains. A follow-up test revealed that the knowledge gains, but not the attitudinal ones, lasted for at least 26 days after the instruction was ended.

165.   Klassen, Frank H., and Donna M. Gollnick (Eds.). Pluralism and the American Teacher. Washington, DC: American Association of Colleges for Teacher Education, 1977.

This volume includes several essays which have been annotated separately. There are also six case studies of multicultural teacher education programs. Five of the programs are in large public universities, and one is a regional center established to assist public schools that were going through the desegregation process. Each description includes a history of the program, an account of the clients it serves, a description of the curricular components, and an assessment of future directions. In some cases, the authors include details about the problems that they encountered in establishing and maintaining these programs.

166. Klassen, Frank H., Donna M. Gollnick, and Kobla I.M.
          Osayande. Multicultural Teacher Education: Guidelines
          for Implementation, volume four. Washington, DC:
          American Association of Colleges for Teacher Education,
          1980.

          The authors describe guidelines for the following
      components of teacher education programs: governance,
      preservice curricula, faculty, students, resources, and
      evaluation. Each guideline is amplified with several
      questions designed to evaluate the degree to which a
      multicultural perspective is reflected in these areas, and
      the extent of its effectiveness. This monograph is designed
      to assist faculty and administrators in assessing their
      current work, and in developing goals for more fully
      implementing a multicultural orientation in their programs.
      There is one major omission in the faculty guidelines:
      recruiting and hiring faculty from diverse backgrounds is
      only mentioned in the discussion of part-time faculty, not
      in the regular faculty.

167. Kohut, Sylvester. "Field Experiences in Preservice
          Professional Studies." Multicultural Teacher
          Education: Preparing Educators to Provide Educational
          Equity. Edited by H. Prentice Baptiste, Mira L.
          Baptiste, and Donna M. Gollnick. Washington, DC:
          American Association of Colleges for Teacher Education,
          1980, 73-93.

          In this chapter, the author offers several ways in
      which field-based and clinical experiences with a
      multicultural orientation can be integrated into all
      professional programs. He suggests that students work in a
      variety of community-based agencies and that colleges
      develop programs such as literacy campaigns that give
      students an opportunity to work with a wide range of people,
      as well as contribute to the local community. Student
      teaching programs in other countries and in a variety of
      communities are other ways in which students can expand
      their knowledge of cultural diversity. He stresses the need
      to support these experiences with seminars and courses.
      Model programs are cited.

168. Landis, Dan, and Richard W. Brislin (Eds.). Handbook of
          Intercultural Training: Volumes 1, 2, 3. New York:
          Pergamon Press, 1983.

These volumes contain numerous papers on a wide range of issues related to intercultural communication. The topics range from specific training techniques to broader issues such as ethics. The third volume has four chapters on intercultural training in educational institutions.

169.   Lee, Marianne. Multicultural Teacher Education: An
       Annotated Bibliography of Selected Resources, volume
       three. Washington, DC: American Association of
       Colleges for Teacher Education, 1980.

This bibliography contains information about books, journals, organizations, and programs concerned with multicultural and bilingual education. Most of the citations are from the middle and late 1970s. The first section includes resources that might be used in planning teacher education courses. They include bibliographies, articles about multicultural education, evaluation guides, material about specific groups, and guidelines and research studies on multicultural education. The second section consists of lists of periodicals that publish multiculturally related articles and potential funding sources. The final section is a compilation of organizations that are concerned with specific cultural groups, or other aspects of multicultural education.

170.   Luke, Allan. "Linguistic Stereotypes, the Divergent Speaker
       and the Teaching of Literacy." Journal of Curriculum
       Studies 18 (1986): 397-408.

Although this article does not address teacher education per se, it does highlight an important issue for teachers that is often misunderstood or neglected in teacher education programs. The author articulates the need for teachers to avoid judging children on the basis of linguistic stereotypes. Instead, they should develop a sensitivity to the culturally specific communication patterns of the children they teach, and incorporate these into their teaching using a whole language or language experience approach. While he emphasizes the need for all children to learn standard English, the author states that this approach will develop children's meta-linguistic awareness of the differences in patterns of speech, and will facilitate their fluency in both ways of speech.

171. Lynch, James. "An Initial Typology of Perspectives on Staff
        Development for Multicultural Teacher Education."
        Multicultural Education: The Interminable Debate.
        Edited by Sohan Modgil, Gajendra K. Verma, Kanka
        Mallick, and Celia Modgil. London: The Falmer Press,
        1986, pp. 149-65.

        In this critique of the current state of multicultural
teacher education in Britain, Lynch points out that efforts
at reforming teacher education have been limited to
individual programs and minor curricular changes. He
proposes a model for faculty and staff development that
employs both Gay's components (knowledge, attitudes, and
skills) and Bank's stages of emerging ethnicity. He
stresses the need for teacher education in Britain to move
from its predominantly ethnocentric orientation to an
institutional and national commitment to multicultural
education.

172. Lynch, James. "Multicultural Education and the Training of
        Teachers: A Case Study." The South Pacific Journal of
        Teacher Education 9 (April 1981): 43-54.

        In this article, Lynch advocates a permeation approach,
rather than an additive one, in terms of reforming teacher
education curriculum to prepare students to teach from a
multicultural perspective. He then describes the program at
Bradford College, Sunderland Polytechnic Institute, England,
that aims to train students to practice emancipatory
education rather than compensatory education. In the first
two years all courses, including social sciences, natural
sciences, and humanities, are taught from a multicultural
perspective and stress both the diversity of human
experience and the common elements of all cultures. In the
third year, students conduct an in-depth study of school
curricula from a multicultural perspective; and, in the
final year, they engage in a critical appraisal of
educational theories and research from a multicultural
perspective. Throughout the four years, students are
involved in classrooms that have children from a variety of
backgrounds. There are also part-time courses for
practicing teachers. This comprehensive program emphasizes
the reciprocal nature of learning, and advocates
"interlearning" between teacher and learner.

173. Mahan, James M., and Warren Lacefield. "Employability and Multi-Cultural Teacher Preparation." _Educational Research Quarterly_ 7 (1982): 15-20.

This account of the development of guidelines for a course in American Indian Studies required of all new teachers in South Dakota articulates some of the dilemmas inherent in training teachers with a multicultural perspective. The author describes the initial tension between providing teachers with information about American Indians that might contribute to a change in attitude, and a focus on usable classroom skills. The resulting guidelines emphasize practical applications, but also include content that familiarizes teachers with both the history and cultural background of specific Native American groups. This course is designed to enable teachers to critically evaluate curricula and to work effectively with Native American families. According to the author, the most important component is the concept of bicultural education, this emphasizes the incorporation of students' backgrounds, rather than the deficit orientation of many compensatory education programs. Citing the works of Paulo Freire and Ivan Illich, the guidelines stress the need for teachers to learn how to stimulate learning in the context of reality as their Indian students experience it.

174. Minister of Supply and Services. _Cross-Cultural Awareness Education and Training for Professionals: A Manual._ Edmonton, Alberta: Department of Education, 1985.

This manual uses a case study method as the basis for a cultural awareness workshop designed for educators and other professionals. By including photographs of the participants and transcripts from speeches, it, in itself, is a case study of how a series of workshops might be conducted. The seven case studies include situations of failed communication, discrimina- tion, or desire for institutional change. They occur in several settings, including a hospital, a union, a school, a police department, and different community organizations. Each case study is described in detail, and followed by suggested discussion guidelines. These are designed to help participants recognize common types of problems that occur over many situations, and the potential impact of individual expectations and the institutional climate.

175. Mitchell, Edna, and Marilyn Watson. "Personal Cultural
        Orientations and Educational Practices." Multicultural
        Teacher Education: Preparing Educators to Provide
        Educational Equity. Edited by H. Prentice Baptiste,
        Mira L. Baptiste, and Donna M. Gollnick. Washington,
        DC: American Association of Colleges for Teacher
        Education, 1980, pp. 154-76.

        In this chapter, the authors describe sources of
   conflict and misunderstanding that can occur when teachers
   and children come from different backgrounds and articulate
   the kinds of information and experiences that teachers
   should have in order to be an effective link between home
   and school. The role of the family, social expectations,
   the style of verbal, nonverbal, and written communications
   in that particular culture, orientation toward time,
   individual learning styles, and family values are
   emphasized.

176. Nixon, Jon. "Teacher Education." A Teacher's Guide to
        Multicultural Education. New York: Basil Blackwell,
        1985, pp. 152-69.

        This book includes a chapter on teacher education that
   is a critique of the current programs in England. The
   author discusses the problems of shifting educational
   policy, lack of diversity among educators at all levels, and
   cynicism of current teaching faculty. He proposes that
   course content at both the preservice and in-service levels
   be designed to induce students to develop both the knowledge
   and the commitment to teach from a multicultural
   perspective.

177. Olstad, R. G., Clifford D. Foster, and Richard M. Wyman.
        "Multicultural Education for Preservice Teachers."
        Integrated Education 21 (1983): 137-39.

        The authors studied the enrollment patterns of 515
   teacher education students who were required to elect one
   course from each of the following categories: (1) the
   broad issues of socioethnic differences, and (2) courses
   that focus on specific socioethnic groups. The enrollment
   patterns suggest that students tend to take courses about
   their own ethnic or social group; hence; this course
   requirement fails to provide a broad multicultural
   perspective. They are especially dismayed at these
   findings, since many universities are attempting to use this

model as a means of incorporating a multicultural
perspective. They suggest as an alternative that
institutions engage in the following process: First, define
multicultural education as it is approved by the
institution; second, involve representatives of diverse
communities in the planning and development process; and
third, generate and implement a systematic plan for
integrating a multicultural perspective in all teacher
education courses.

178. Paley, Vivian Gussin. White Teacher. Cambridge, MA:
       Harvard University Press, 1979.

       This personal account of a white teacher of an
ethnically mixed kindergarten provides many insights into
the process of teachers recognizing and dealing with subtle
forms of prejudice. Written in a journalistic style, the
book includes numerous observations of children's peer
interactions, and their contacts with their teacher.
Paley's commentary describes her reactions, perceptions, and
changes. This volume might be used effectively to stimulate
teacher education students' discussion about their own
feelings.

179. Ramsey, Patricia G. Teaching and Learning in a Diverse
       World: Multicultural Education for Young Children.
       New York: Teachers College Press, 1987.

       This book contains one chapter that addresses
specifically teacher's readines to implement a multicultural
perspective. Suggestions include exercises, questions, and
experiences designed to help students or practicing teachers
identify and challenge their own attitudes, and learn more
about the community and the specific children with whom they
work. Throughout the book there is an emphasis on teachers'
questioning their assumptions and critiquing the curriculum
from a multicultural perspective.

180. Renwick, George W. Evaluation Handbook for Cross-Cultural
       Training and Multicultural Education. LaGrange Park,
       IL: Intercultural Network, Inc., 1980.

       This monograph describes a variety of instruments that
can be used to assess the effectiveness of cross-cultural
training. The areas of assessment include cultural
knowledge attained, changes in perceptions and attitudes,

the acquisition of skills, and changes in specific
interpersonal and intercultural behaviors. The methods
include direct questions, checklists, written exercises,
projective techniques, journals, observations, and
evaluations of particular parts of the training. There are
also guidelines for tabulating and interpreting the results.
These procedures might be adapted to assess education
students' readiness to work in multicultural settings and
the effectiveness of specific components of the preparation
program.

181. Robinson, Gail L. Nemetz. Crosscultural Understanding. New
         York: Pergamon Institute of English, 1985.

To emphasize the complexity of culture, the author
discusses its many visible and invisible aspects, and the
multiple and subtle ways in which it influences perceptions
of ourselves and others. One chapter discusses the
acquistion of culture and cultural roles, and two others
deal explicitly with forming positive perceptions of other
groups and modifying negative ones. The book concludes with
a discussion of the cognitive and attitudinal aspects of a
multicultural orientation. Throughout this volume, the
author integrates psychological theories and research with
practical applications.

182. Rodriguez, Fred. Mainstreaming a Multicultural Concept into
         Teacher Education: Guidelines for Teacher Training.
         Saratoga, CA: R & E Publishers, 1983.

In this practical guide, the author discusses some of
the impediments to incorporating a multicultural orientation
into teacher preparation programs, such as conflicts among
faculty and programs, conflicts between teacher education
programs and local schools, and faculty resistance. He
describes specific activities to engage faculty in the
process of analyzing the current program and setting goals
to increase its multicultural orientation. The book
contains several instruments for assessing programs and
materials and defining personal and departmental goals.
There is a model workshop designed to facilitate these
processes. The volume concludes with a comprehensive list
of books, libraries, periodicals, and organizations that are
potential resources for teachers and teacher educators.

183.   Saracho, Olivia N., and Bernard Spodek.   "Preparing Teachers
           for Multicultural Classrooms." Understanding the
           Multicultural Experience in Early Childhood Education.
           Edited by Olivia N. Saracho and Bernard Spodek.
           Washington, DC: National Association for the Education
           of Young Children, 1983, pp.125-46.

       This work describes how teacher education should be
    modified to integrate a multicultural perspective into the
    following six components: recruitment and selection of
    prospective teachers, general education, professional
    foundations, instructional knowledge, practice, and program
    evaluation and modification.

184.   Saville-Troike, Muriel. A Guide to Culture in the
           Classroom. Roslyn, VA: National Clearinghouse for
           Bilingual Education, 1978.

       This monograph discusses several aspects of cultural
    influences on learning and identity. The author cautions
    the reader about the prevalence of unfounded assumptions
    about members of particular cultures, and provides a
    comprehensive list of questions for educators to use to
    learn information for themselves about specific cultures and
    individuals who are members of the group. The author also
    discusses the need for teachers to know sensitive ways of
    learning about cultural differences and teaching children
    from many groups.

185.   Sims, William E. "Preparing Teachers for Multicultural
           Classrooms." Momentum 14 (February 1983): 42-44.

       In this article, Sims advocates the infusion method of
    curriculum reform, rather than the addition of one or two
    courses, as a means of meeting the NCATE requirement. He
    argues that this approach is both more effective and
    economical, and demonstrates how the traditional sequence of
    teacher preparation courses could be adapted to incorporate
    a multicultural perspective. He also lists specific
    multicultural teaching competencies.

186.   Sims, William E., and Bernice Bass de Martinez.
           Perspectives in Multicultural Education. New York:
           University Press of America, 1981.

At the conclusion of this book, the authors provide
examples of lesson plans that were developed by students in
a seminar in multicultural education. There are also sample
plans to disseminate a multicultural perspective in other
schools and districts.

187.   Sitaram, K.S., and Roy T. Cogdell. Foundations of
          Intercultural Communication. Columbus, OH: Charles E.
          Merrill, 1976.

       This text covers the major components of intercultural
communication that include the ways in which people perceive
the world, retain information, express ideas (both verbally
and nonverbally), acquire value systems, and construct
social institutions. Many examples are included to
illustrate how poor cross- cultural understanding can
disrupt communication.

188.   Watson, Keith. "Training Teachers in the United Kingdom for
          a Multicultural Society - The Rhetoric and the
          Reality." Journal of Multilingual and Multicultural
          Development 5 (1984): 385-400.

       This critique of British teacher education articulates
reasons why so little has changed since the 1970s. The
author cites the lack of government support and a clear
policy for multicultural education. He attributes the
persistent ethnocentrism on the part of teachers to the fact
that multicultural education and related issues are
peripheral to most teacher education programs.

189.   Williams, Leslie R., Yvonne De Gaetano, Iris R. Sutherland,
          and Charles C. Harrington. ALERTA: A Multicultural,
          Bilingual Approach to Teaching Young Children.
          Reading, MA: Addison-Wesley, 1985.

       This book contains several specific activities for
staff development and preparation to implement the ALERTA
Program. The emphasis is on sharing one's own background,
and developing good communication skills and teamwork within
a staff at a school or a center.

CHAPTER V

FUTURE DIRECTIONS IN MULTICULTURAL EDUCATION

Edwina B. Vold, Leslie R. Williams
and Patricia G. Ramsey

A multicultural perspective on education has evolved out of
periods of crisis and controversy in the United States and other
western societies. It is an educational perspective which
denounces institutionalized racism perpertrated against particular
racial and ethnic groups, and the resulting social, economic and
educational inequities these groups experience. The goals of
multicultural education are, thus, to reduce racism, to design
systems of education that are inclusive rather than exclusive, and
to provide an equitable way for all students to enter the
mainstream possessing the skills for social and economic success.

Socio-Political Dimensions Revisited

This perspective on multicultural education is in itself a
source of conflict and is embedded in controversy in the late
1980s. Arguments against the multicultural perspective and
against the social ideology on which it is based are woven
throughout educational literature and are debated at major
educational conferences and symposia. Although there seems to be
no shortage of criticism, the one most often raised is that, in
its attempt to heighten awareness of racial and ethnic identities,
multicultural education proves to be divisive. Critics claim that
pluralism as an ideology contains the seeds of separatism,
aggravating problems for societies that are already characterized
by racial fragmentation (Pratte, 1977; Serow, 1983).
Critics who are themselves members of minority groups, have
also argued against multicultural education. They remark on the
naivite of the assumption that a single educational movement can
bring about change in society which is steeped in a monocultural

and Angloconforming tradition. Serow (1983) agrees with these
critics and notes that the racial system in the United States is
so well entrenched that it is beyond the reach of the limited
goals of multicultural education. Influenced by conservative
Black writers like Sowell (1972) Serow goes even further to
suggest that multicultural education harms minority children. He
says:

> Since American society is unlikely to have changed
> substantially by the time the alumni of today's ethnic
> studies courses graduate, it seems pointless, even cruel to
> some observers to provide children with skills and
> orientations for a pluralistic society that does not and will
> not exist. Thus, multicultural education is ... seen as
> distracting from the real needs of minority students. (p.
> 102)

Ramsey (1987) devotes much of the last chapter of her book to
responses to criticism of multicultural education. She posits
that some of the arguments reflect a misunderstanding of the
goals, while others raise legitimate concerns. The criticisms
cited focus on the isolating influences of multicultural
education, and the tendency of groups to resegregate themselves.
Arguments related to the feasibility issue raise such questions
as, "Can educators and children...actually solve such complex
problems as racism and discrimination?" Another argument against
multicultural education considers whether multicultural education
detracts from the acquisition of the basic academic skills needed
by children of all racial and ethnic groups. Ramsey's responses
to each of the criticisms provide the reader with practical ways
of debating key issues.

Many of these criticisms reflect the lack of agreement among
proponents of multicultural education regarding appropriate
terminology (See Chapter I). Differing terminologies do reflect
some differences in the expected outcomes. Since articulation of
the outcomes anticipated for multicultural education is maintaining the movement's momentum, consideration of expected outcomes
may help to clarify the debate.

The literature reveals intended outcomes that range from what
is expected for the individual, to what is expected for schools
and for society as a whole. The outcomes for the individual focus
on maximizing individual potential and furnishing the individual
with a sense of self, a sense of belonging, and a sense of worth,
while decreasing any sense of ethnic superiority. The expected
outcomes for schools are, most particularly, symbolic and
functional acceptance of diversity. Symbolic acceptance is a
process in which students acquire favorable attitudes toward the
hypothetical representation of political or ethnic diversity, such

as support for the principles of civil liberties or racial
equality. Functional acceptance, on the other hand, creates
conditions whereby members of diverse groups in schools are
willing and able to work together in pursuit of shared goals. It
reflects a belief that all members of a society benefit from a
multicultural education perspective when its members attain
socioeconomic mobility (Serow, 1983).

The Socioeconomic mobility of ethnic groups is crucial when
we consider the long-term demographic trends of this country.
Hodgkinson (1985) has predicted that by the year 2000, one-third
of the population of the United States will be non-white. Given
the age distribution, the percentage of "minority" children in
schools will be even higher. These statistics add a particular
note of urgency to the need to make schools more responsive to and
accepting of diversity. We must find ways to educate effectively
children from a range of racial, cultural, linguistic, and class
backgrounds.

In the late 1980s, there are policy issues that also must be
addressed, if multicultural education is to remain a viable
educational construct. More attention must be paid to the
politics affecting education. Schools in the United States have
been influenced by the collective political force of blacks, and
later, of other "minority" groups. Underlying their struggle was
the push for political control, as well as educational equity.
Through active lobbying, policies emerged which forced
institutional changes in the way blacks and others were to be
educated, and in the content of curriculum, although most of the
resulting curricula have remained supplementary.

Taking the next step, that is, implementing an infusion
approach to multicultural education, entails a commitment by
teachers and administrators that exceeds that required by any
other educational movement in this century. It requires a change
in attitudes as well as that teachers, administrators and teacher
educators will model such things as equitable treatment of
students and respect for diversity. This demonstration implies
moving beyond the stage of rhetoric that has characterized most
policy statements, to a clear plan of action.

That plan of action must encompass at least three components:
(1) continuing attention to refinement of multicultural
educational programs, curricula, and teaching strategies; (2)
infusion of teacher education programs with a multicultural
perspective; and (3) pursuit of research that qualitatively (as
well as quantitatively) studies the effectiveness of multicultural
education, and thus addresses criticisms of the movement.

Refinement of Educational Resources

Review of the available resources on multicultural programs, curricula and teaching strategies has revealed the significance in the minds of materials developers of recognition of the contexts of human learning. At the conclusion of Chapter III, the notion of context was introduced, alluding to all of the physical, psychological, and social dimensions that serve simultaneously as the background and the impetus for human development.

"Contexts" are the collective experiences that children bring with them to school, and subsequently use to interpret what they are taught. Where children have been raised, the objects, events, and people that have been a part of their lives, the values and beliefs that have been transmitted to them by those who care for them, together constitute powerful frames of reference. Whether or not what is learned in school makes sense to children or is considered viable by them depends on how well the new information or skills relate to their previous understandings of their world. Where little or no relationship appears to exist, academic content and skills may be rejected as irrelevant.

The importance of relating to the contexts of children's ongoing lives, of personalizing the curriculum so that children may view it within their frames of reference, has been an implicit theme in the development of multicultural educational materials and resources. The theme is related to the premises undergirding multicultural materials development. These premises appear to have been drawn for the most part, from classic child developmental and educational literature. In brief, they are:

1. Children bring with them to the learning circumstance a repertoire of knowledge, skills and attitudes acquired through engagement with their families, communities, and cultures. These experiential repertoires should be used as the foundations for subsequent learning (Dewey, 1938; Erikson, 1951).

2. Children are active constructors of their own intelligence. Their ongoing construction draws strongly on both their individual (psychological) and group (social, cultural) experience through direct interaction with the people, objects, and events in their environment (Piaget & Inhelder, 1969). Such activity implies the use of multiple modes of representation of knowledge (enactive, iconic, symbolic as defined by Bruner, 1968) and multiple modalities (visual, auditory, kinesthetic).

3. Children learn most easily and with most lasting effect when learning is personalized, that is, directly related to their experience. This relationship should be made

through both affective and cognitive connections (Isaacs, 1972).

4. The contexts of human learning (as perviously defined) are, therefore, vitally important. The more immediately recognizable the context, the more likely will the children be able to assimilate and accommodate the new material (Dewey, 1938; Piaget & Inhelder, 1962).

5. Learning involves social, as well as individual construction of knowledge (Vygotsky, 1962). As attribution of meaning to experience is often mediated through contact with peers and adults, collaborative and cooperative teaching strategies are likely to be effective in promoting new knowledge, skills, and attitudes.

6. The pathway to social change lies in attention to individuals within an educational setting that actively promotes the desired change (Freire, 1970).

Using these premises as points of departure, developers have frequently created materials that focus on maximizing individual potential, but fail to address the larger, structural changes that must occur in society. The intended outcomes, ranging from improvement of academic performance to symbolic and functional acceptance of diversity, assume that changes in the attitudes and behavior of individuals will ultimately lead to change in society as a whole. Yet, we can surmise from study of the history of the multicultural education movement, that individual efforts will remain limited in their impact unless educational policies at the local, state, and national levels are instituted and implemented in the public schools.

The implications of this projection are that multicultural educational materials and resources in the future should include presentation of the content and skills needed for participation in the political process. Children of all ages should be encouraged to consider issues of equity, whether around the decision of who should be first in line for a kindergarten outing, or who should ensure equal exposure of the candidates for a high school class election. At each developmental level, children need to become increasingly aware of how diversity of perspectives affects group decisions, and be helped to make more informed and humane choices. These are the seeds of policy making.

Thus, future work in program/curriculum refinement should involve movement toward connecting educational processes with the possibilities for social change, or what Sleeter and Grant (1987) would term the "social reconstructionist" point of view. At the same time, the materials should continue to embody awareness and use of the particular contexts that affect human learning, as ways of guiding the formation of positive attitudes and behavior toward others.

No program, curriculum, or teaching strategy will be ultimately successful, however, unless attention is paid to the preparation of those persons responsible for implementing it. The real key to change may lie in teacher education.

Reorientation of Teacher Education Programs

Goals of Multicultural Teacher Education

As discussed in Chapter IV, the goals of multicultural teacher education include affective, cognitive, and informational dimensions. Their achievement will require a comprehensive and profound reorientation of all aspects of teacher preparation programs. As the reviews and critiques have shown, simply exposing students to the concept of multicultural education is not sufficient. Experiences that challenge students' basic social assumptions and broaden their informational and attitudinal perspectives must be included. This process is articulated in the following goals that are derived from the numerous works discussed and annotated in Chapter IV.

First, teacher education programs should provide opportunities for students to articulate their assumptions about their own and other groups of people and to engage in experiences that challenge misconceptions and broaden their range of knowledge. To accomplish this goal, course work should include experiences such as films, field trips, guest speakers, and sustained contact with members of other groups.

Second, students should learn about the historical and contemporary experiences and contributions of diverse groups in this country, especially those that have had histories of being oppressed. Liberal arts requirements should include courses in the arts, anthropology, sociology, social history, and political science that critically examine the relationships among racial, cultural, gender, and class groups in this country and between the United States and other nations. Child development courses should incorporate a cross-cultural perspective and a critique of the deficit-oriented research that has often concluded that 'minority' groups are inadequate. Because most disciplines have an inherent pro-Western orientation, courses should be scrutinized continuously to insure that they present a variety of perspectives.

Third, foundations courses should emphasize the ways in which education often supports the status quo and the existing hierarchy. For example, courses on testing might include information about cultural and linguistic bias of tests and the ways in which they often are used to support discriminatory educational practices. Students also should learn how to critique curricula for cultural bias and to observe ways in which school and curricula perpetuate discriminatory attitudes and practices.

Fourth, courses should include experiences that help students develop a clear philosophy of education that embodies a respect for all people and a commitment to contribute to social change. Carl Grant (1983) has emphasized the need for students to enter the field with a clear set of values and priorities so that "they do not end up applauding or defending what they are doing simply because it is convenient, but because they...believe in it" (p. 30).

Fifth, courses and field experiences should be designed to ensure that students develop skills in working with children and families from a variety of backgrounds. By the time they have completed the program, students should know how to gain relevant information about families, cultures, and communities so that they can be effective in working with their specific groups of children. Basic methods courses should include guidelines on adapting materials and teaching styles so that teachers can be effective with a wide range of children (Gay, 1983). Students should have opportunities to observe and critique their interactions with children from different backgrounds (Kleifgen, 1987). Their preparation should also include experiences in helping children negotiate the differences between their home cultures and school demands. This "cultural brokering" (Gentemann and Whitehead, 1983) can ease the transition from home to school and prevent miscommunication that often leads to failure.

Sixth, programs should provide information and experiences that insure that all students know how to teach about diversity and how to impart a multicultural perspective throughout the curriculum. Child development courses should include information on the development of racial and ethnic attitudes so that teachers know how to convey concepts of diversity in age-appropriate and situation-appropriate ways. Skills in fostering intergroup acceptance and incorporating a broad cultural perspective should be emphasized in teacher preparation courses and field experiences.

The Implementation of Multicultural
Teacher Education Programs

Because of its comprehensive nature, implementing multicultural teacher education requires a broad assessment and profound reform of all aspects of teacher preparation programs. The most obvious factor in any educational reform is the faculty. First, serious recruitment efforts should be employed to increase the numbers of minority faculty, and any new faculty should be

selected for their commitment to multicultural education. In
terms of existing faculty, Gollnick, Osaysande, and Levy (1980)
suggest that administrators can create incentives and development
programs to encourage the acquisition of skills and knowledge
related to multicultural education. According to Rodriguez
(1983), these programs should include opportunities for faculty to
discuss and resolve their resistances to incorporating this
perspective so that they can approach programmatic change with a
genuine commitment.

The recruitment and retention of potential teachers and
students of education from diverse backgrounds is a particular
priority for several reasons. First, it is incumbent upon
institutions to practice educational equity in all of their
policies regarding admission. Second, we must prepare significant
numbers of teachers from diverse backgrounds so that the schools
will have more multicultural staffs. Third, the presence of
'minority' students in teacher preparation programs creates a more
genuinely multicultural learning environment for all students.
However, as Grant, Sabol and Sleeter (1980) point out, the entry
of non-traditional students requires careful assessment and
redesign of policies and programs related to recruitment,
admissions, retention and post-graduate placement.

These efforts require the involvement of other departments,
the institution as a whole, and the community. Curriculum reform
affects not only education courses, but courses in all
departments, especially those that provide foundation courses for
education students. Kohut (1980) suggests that interdepartmental
liaisons and cross-disciplinary committees be established to
implement these changes and to avoid territorial disputes. Too
often educational reforms do not reflect the real needs of the
people affected by them. Gollnick et al., (1980) point out that,
in order to develop the most effective programs, the communities
from which students come and those where they go to teach should
be involved in the planning and implementation of teacher
education reform.

Current Challenges and Future Directions
in Multicultural Teacher Education

Currently there are many reform movements in teacher
education. The Holmes Group Report (1986) and the Carnegie
Commission Report (1986) have spawned numerous new certification
regulations and programs at both the state and federal level.
Many of the reformers emphasize the need to train teachers to be
more effective with "minority" children. At the same time, none
of these documents specifically mentions multicultural education.
In fact, with the renewed emphasis on "traditional" disciplines

and Western culture, they may inhibit efforts to infuse a
multicultural perspective into all areas of teacher education.
They also emphasize the need to "professionalize" teaching.
Higher salaries and more autonomy are laudable goals and may help
to attract and retain more minority teachers. However, the Holmes
Report, in particular, argues that teacher education be limited to
graduate schools and eliminated from undergraduate programs. This
plan threatens to reduce further the numbers of teachers from
minority backgrounds as well as those from low-SES families.

Instead of simply complying with these critiques, educators
and institutions need to take advantage of the current public
interest in teacher preparation to demand resources for reforming
programs so that they will be authentically multicultural in their
personnel, structure and curricula. One clear priority is to
develop research strategies that can accurately evaluate
multicultural teacher education programs and assist in setting
priorities and gaining public support for these reforms. As
discussed in the next section, this endeavor requires moving
beyond the linear and quantitative methods that traditionally have
been used in educational research.

Future Directions for Research in Multicultural Education

The expanded vision of the goals of multicultural education,
and the projected reorientation of teacher education programs
suggest a variety of research questions to guide future
investigations. Among them are:

- What individual and environmental actions influence the
  development of ethnic and social attitudes and identities?
  How does this interaction change as children pass through
  stages of cognitive, affective, and social development?
- What relationship, if any, exists between teaching style,
  learning style, and achievement?
- What kinds of learning materials and/or teaching
  strategies promote cross-cultural (cross-ethnic, cross-
  racial) interactions among individuals?
- What kinds of learning materials and/or teaching
  strategies promote positive changes in attitude and/or
  behavior of individuals toward members of groups other
  than their own?
- What teaching/learning contexts promote exercise of social
  problem-solving skills?
- What relationship, if any, exists between the orientation
  of a program of teacher education and teachers' incorporation of a multicultural perspective in their work?

A distinctive feature of research questions such as these is demonstration of their awareness of the transactional nature of human development and the teaching and learning processes. They reveal that the phenomena under consideration are understood to be interactive, and can be studied accurately only in relation to the settings in which they appear. Context once again becomes a vital factor in the teasing out of possible effects. Yet context has not been a major consideration in many classic educational studies. Instead, research designs have favored the experimental models drawn from some branches of psychology.

The linear and quantitatively based methods traditionally used in educational research are increasingly being considered to be too limited in their pursuit of "clean" results, however. Investigators of program effects note that the goals of multicultural education are multidimensional, and require a combination of rigorously applied qualitative and quantitative methods to capture the dynamic associated with particular results.

If multicultural programs, curricula, and teaching strategies, and concomitant programs of teacher education are to gain strength over the coming decade, and if multicultural education is to present itself as a viable alternative to existing systems, such research must be actively addressed in the near future. Federal and philanthropic monies should be sought for scholarly investigation of program effects using contextually sensitive methods. Without such a reorientation and sharpening of research methods, and their application in the field of multicultural education, further development in the movement may be in jeopardy.

Conclusion

Demographic studies reveal that the population of American society will be drastically different in the 1990s. Although the United States has made some progress toward achieving the goals of multicultural education, there can be no assumption that genuine and constructive recognition of cultural pluralism exists. There is still a lack of equity for many of society's racial and ethnic minorities, at the same time as many new groups are arriving in the United States. Many of these new arrivals come from third world countries. While they bring to North American schools some of the same behaviors and needs as those of minority children already present, they also bring additional values, customs and languages not prized in many classrooms in the United States. So, the problem of providing equity for all is becoming increasingly prominent in our schools.

Since schools have been delegated the task of formally transmitting the values, customs, and language of a common population, policies and practices that affect what actually occurs in schools must be addressed. Schools must acknowledge the value of individualism at the same time as they promote the concept of cultural pluralism. Any educational policies and practices created must address this dual concern.

Discussions about what schools can and should transmit will remain political in nature. Whatever decisions are made regarding multicultural education will be based upon awareness of prevailing societal beliefs and behavior, and the elements and pressures behind them (Pizzillo, 1983). Awareness, however, is only the first step. The collective pressure of racial and ethnic minorities, and of educators committed to educational equity, will be the only way to move our schools to the reality of incorporation of a multicultural perspective into the educational process.

References

A Nation Prepared: Teachers for the Twenty-First Century. The
   Report of the Carnegie Forum on Education and the Economy's
   Task Force on Teaching as a Profession. Washington, DC: The
   Forum, 1986.

Berghe, Van Den, Pierre. *Race and Racism: Comparative
   Perspective.* New York: Wiley, 1978.

Bowles, Samuel and Herbert Gintis. *Schooling in Capitalist
   America.* New York: Basic, 1976.

Bruner, Jerome. *Toward a Theory of Instruction.* New York: W. W.
   Norton, 1968.

Dewey, John. *Experience and Education.* New York: Macmillan,
   1938.

Erickson, Erik. *Childhood and Society.* New York: Norton, 1951.

Freire, Paolo. *Pedagogy of the Oppressed.* New York: Seabury,
   1970.

Gay, Geneva. "Why Multicultural Education in Teacher Preparation
   Programs." *Contemporary Education* 54 (1983): 79-85.

Gentemann, Karen M., and Tony L. Whitehead. "The Cultural Broker
   Concept in Bicultural Education." *Journal of Negro Education*
   52 (1983): 118-29.

Gollnick, Donna M., Kobla I.M. Osayande, and Jack Levy.
   *Multicultural Teacher Education: Case Studies of Thirteen
   Programs.* Washington, D.C.: American Association of
   Colleges for Colleges for Teacher Education, 1980.

Grant, Carl A. "Multicultural Teacher Education - Renewing the
   Discussion: A Response to Martin Haberman." *Journal of
   Teacher Education* 34 (March-April 1983): 29-32.

rant, Carl A., Ruth Sabol, and Christine E. Sleeter. "Recruitment, Admissions, Retention, and Placement for Educational Equity: An Analysis of the Process." Multicultural Teacher Education: Preparing Educators to Provide Educational Equity. Edited by H. Prentice Baptiste, Mira L. Baptiste, and Donna M. Gollnick. Washington, D.C.: American Association of Colleges for Teacher Education, 1980, pp. 7-43.

Hodgkinson, Harold L. All One System: Demographics of Education, Kindergarten through Graduate School. Washington, D.C.: Institute for Educational Leadership, Inc., 1985.

Issacs, Susan. Intellectual Growth in Young Children. New York: Schocken, 1972.

Kleifgen, Jo Ann. What can be Learned from Student-Teachers' Cross-Cultural Communicative Failures? Paper presented at the annual meeting of the American Educational Research Association, Washington, D.C. April, 1987.

Kohut, Sylvester. "Field Experiences in Preservice Professional Studies." Multicultural Teacher Education: Preparing Education to Provide Educational Equity. Edited by H. Prentice Baptiste, Mira L. Baptiste and Donna M. Gollnick Washington, D.C.: American Association of Colleges for Teacher Education, 1980, 73-93.

Lynch, James. "Multiethnic Education in Europe: Problems and Prospects." Phi Delta Kappan 64, 1983: 576-579.

Piaget, Jean, and Barbel Inhelder. The Psychology of the Child. New York: Basic Books, 1969.

Pizzillo, Jr. Joseph J. Intercultural Studies: Schooling and Diversity. Iowa: Kendall/Hunt, 1983.

Pratte, Richard. "Cultural Diversity and Education." Ethnic and Educational Policy. Edited by K. Strike and K. Egan. London: Routledge and Kegan Paul, 1978.

Ramsey, Patricia. Teaching and Learning in a Diverse World: Multicultural Education for Young Children. New York: Teachers College Press, 1987.

Rodriguez, Fred. Mainstreaming a Multicultural Concept into Teacher Education: Guidelines for Teacher Training. Saratoga, CA: R & E Publishers, 1983.

Serow, Robert. Schooling for Diversity: An Analysis of Policy
    and Practice. New York: Teachers College Press, 1983.

Sleeter, Christine E., and Carl A. Grant. "An Analysis of
    Multicultural Education in the United States." Harvard
    Educational Review 57 (1987): 421-44.

Sowell, Thomas. Black education: Myths and Tragedies. New York:
    McKay, 1972.

Tomorrow's Teachers: A Report of The Holmes Group. The Holmes
    Group, Inc., 501 Erickson Hall, East Lansing, MI 48824-1034,
    1986.

Vygotsky, Lev Semenovich. Thought and Language. Cambridge, MA:
    The M.I.T. Press, 1962.